"Scholars and students have long needed an accessible version of the *Life of Hypatius*, and Storin's skillful translation brings the life of this late ancient saint into elegant, striking English. The scenes in Hypatius's life illustrate major themes in the study of early Christianity, from the importance of bodily holiness to the prevalence of religious violence, from the basic tenets of spiritual direction to the organization of a successful monastery. Accompanying the text is a comprehensive introduction to Hypatius's life and to the late ancient genre of saints' lives in general—teachers and students will benefit from Storin's sensible, erudite treatment of hagiography and its uses."

> — Ellen Muehlberger, professor of history, University of Michigan

"In his translation of this understudied text, Storin shares the foundational narratives of a monastery in a suburb of fifth-century Constantinople. While very much hagiography with all its tropes, the text also reveals the workings of a significant monastery involved in the ecclesiastical disputes of its days, as well as its role in a late antique neighborhood with all its peculiar characters, squabbles, and worries. It is a delightful text that offers valuable glimpses into how the relationship between a local monastery and its community were imagined."

> — Rebecca Stephens Falcasantos, assistant professor of religion, Amherst College

CISTERCIAN STUDIES SERIES:
NUMBER THREE HUNDRED ONE

Callinicus

The Life of Our Sacred Father, Hypatius of the Rufinianae

Translation and Introduction by
Bradley K. Storin

Cistercian Publications
cistercianpublications.org

LITURGICAL PRESS
Collegeville, Minnesota
litpress.org

A Cistercian Publications title published by Liturgical Press

Cistercian Publications
Editorial Offices
161 Grosvenor Street
Athens, Ohio 45701
cistercianpublications.org

Cover art courtesy of Dreamstime.com.

Translated from G. J. M. Bartelink. *Callinicos. Vie d'Hypatios.* Sources chrétiennes 177. Paris: Éditions du Cerf, 1971.

Biblical quotations are translated by the book's translator.

Library of Congress Cataloging-in-Publication Data

Names: Callinicus, Monk of Rufinianae, active 447-450 author. | Storin, Bradley K., translator, writer of introduction.
Title: The life of our sacred father, Hypatius of the Rufinianae / Callinicus ; translation and introduction by Bradley K. Storin.
Other titles: Vios tou hosiou patros hëmön Hypatiou tou en Rouphinianais. English
Description: Collegeville, Minnesota : Cistercian Publications : Liturgical Press, [2025] | Series: Cistercian studies series ; number 301 | Based on three manuscripts: Vaticanus graecus 1667 (10th cent.), Parisinus graecus 1488 (11th cent.), and Athoniensis Philotheou 8 (11th cent.). | Includes bibliographical references and indexes. | Summary: "Better known by its short title, the Life of Hypatius was written in the mid-fifth century by Callinicus, the second abbot of the monastery that Hypatius (ca. 366-446) founded across the Bosporus Strait from Constantinople. Saint Hypatius was known for his ascetic regimen, unflagging rigor, and spiritual wisdom. In this monastic hagiography, readers encounter a vision where monks are spiritual enforcers working to promote Christian orthodoxy, worship, and moral conduct"— Provided by publisher.
Identifiers: LCCN 2024030422 (print) | LCCN 2024030423 (ebook) | ISBN 9780879073565 (trade paperback) | ISBN 9780879073596 (epub) | ISBN 9780879073619 (pdf)
Subjects: LCSH: Hypatius, Saint, approximately 366-446. | Manuscripts, Greek. | Manuscripts, French.
Classification: LCC BR1720.H9 C3313 2025 (print) | LCC BR1720.H9 (ebook) | DDC 270.1—dc23/eng/20240823
LC record available at https://lccn.loc.gov/2024030422
LC ebook record available at https://lccn.loc.gov/2024030423

Contents

Acknowledgments

I would like to thank Marsha Dutton, who enthusiastically accepted this translation into Cistercian Studies. With her eagle eye, she kept many syntactical errors, infelicitous phrasings, inconsistencies of tense, and dangling participles from seeing the light of day. The project is all the better for her energetic involvement.

Louisiana State University, as ever, has been a generous supporter of my research agenda. This manuscript came to completion during a much-appreciated sabbatical in the spring of 2024, granted by Dean Troy Blanchard in the College of Humanities and Social Sciences. I remain ever grateful to the colleagues and undergraduate students I have here at LSU, many of whom have been a sounding-board for anything related to Hypatius. The students in my HNRS 2030, "Holy Violence in Early Christianity," and HNRS 2030, "The Lives of Saints," seminars deserve special thanks for lively discussions of monkish roughhousing and hagiographical spectacles.

Special thanks to Mark DelCogliano, who read through my translation side by side with the critical edition and provided me with invaluable annotations on how to better render the Greek in many places. Additionally, I would like to thank Ellen K. Muehlberger, who read through the translation and offered suggestions for how to make improvements. There is no grander boon than having good friends who just happen to be excellent translators and world-renowned experts on Christianity in late antiquity.

As ever, for making my life a happy one, I thank the loves of my life, my wife Suzannah Edgar and our daughters Corrina and Ruby.

Constantinople and the Surrounding Area

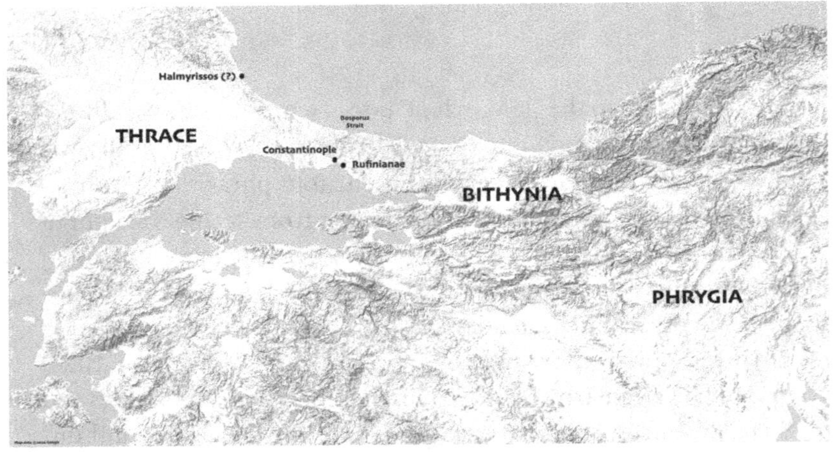

Introduction

This is the story of a little-known "suburban saint"[1] who established a mid-sized monastery just across the Bosporus from Constantinople, one of the largest and most politically important urban centers in the late Roman, or early Byzantine, world. Born to a well-off family that could afford to send him through a costly education in literature and rhetoric in the province of Phrygia (southeast of Constantinople and Bithynia), Hypatius went to church one day when he was eighteen years old and heard the voice of Jesus in Matthew 19:29 calling for true disciples to abandon father and mother, sisters and brothers, spouse and children, and all possessions and to follow him. Hypatius's response to these words could not have been more drastic: he left everything and traveled across Phrygia, Bithynia, and Constantinople before settling in Thrace, where he found a church in which he could live a quietly pious ascetic life. Twenty years later, Hypatius joined a nearby community of ascetics led by a certain Jonah but then left after two years there to assist his father with a legal matter. His father soon died, and, rather than return to Thrace, Hypatius traveled back across the Bosporus with two new friends, Timothy and Moschius. Together they searched for an isolated spot where they could practice asceticism. The trio did not have to go far, for they came across an abandoned monastery on an estate known

[1] Cyril Mango, "Saints," in *The Byzantines* (Chicago: University of Chicago Press, 1997), 275. For the only comprehensive study of the text that I know of, see Eugen Wölfle, *Hypatios, Leben und Bedeutung des Abtes von Rufiniane*, Europäische Hochschulschriften 23 (Frankfurt am Main: Peter Lang, 1986).

as the Rufinianae, just south of Chalcedon. There Hypatius established a monastic community that grew to fifty members; he remained there for roughly four decades until his death.

All the information above comes from the monastic hagiography translated here—*The Life of Our Sacred Father, Hypatius of the Rufinianae* or, simply, the *Life of Hypatius*. Its importance stems from its being the earliest internal text native to the monastic movements in and around Constantinople during the fourth and fifth centuries.[2] Written in the mid-fifth century, it describes its protagonist's activity back to the first decade of the fifth century.

Other sources, however—chronologically, geographically, or simply contextually distant from the *Life of Hypatius*—shed some light on monastic movements in and around Constantinople during the fourth century. The first ascetic activist in the region was Marathonius, a former soldier who oversaw the capital city's charitable establishments and who participated in the Homoiousian movement alongside the bishops Eustathius of Sebaste and Macedonius of Constantinople.[3] Each bishop regarded the Holy Spirit as an instrument of God rather than as a full participant in the divine Trinity, a theological commitment that led to their depositions at the Council of Constantinople 360, and each bishop veered toward radicalism in his own right. Eustathius's ascetic program, for instance, discouraged ownership of private property, encouraged women to cut their hair, prodded slaves to reject bondage, and denied some aspects of ecclesiastical authority and liturgy, while Macedonius, it seems, used physical violence against his

---

[2] Gilbert Dagron, "Le monachisme à Constantinople jusqu'au concile de Chalcédoine (451)," *Travaux et mémoires* 4 (1970): 229–76: "Parmi les *Vies* de saints moines qui se rattachent géographiquement à Constantinople et historiquement aux IVe et Ve siècles, seule celle d'Hypatios est tenue généralement pour digne de foi" (231).

[3] See Sozomen, *Ecclesiastical History* 4.27.4. See Susanna Elm, *"Virgins of God": The Making of Asceticism in Late Antiquity*, Oxford Classical Monographs (Oxford: Clarendon Press, 1994), 106–31. See also R. P. C. Hanson, *The Search for the Christian Doctrine of God: The Arian Controversy, 318–381* (London and New York: T&T Clark, 1988), 760–62.

adversaries.[4] When Marathonius's allies were deposed—Eustathius at the Council of Gangra in 358 and Macedonius at the Council of Constantinople in 360—he and his monks seem to have disappeared from Constantinople.[5]

It took the arrival of three immigrants, all mentioned in the *Life of Hypatius*, to revive organized ascetic activity in the area. The first was Isaac, who came from Syria and established the Monastery of Dalmatios (named after Isaac's successor). Rumor had it that he prophesied the death of the Homoian Emperor Valens in 378 and, as a result, built up a base of support among pro-Nicenes.[6] The later hagiography of Isaac offers little biographical or historical information other than the simple fact that he initiated the first coenobitic community in the capital, but the church historian Sozomen portrays him as an adversary of and contributor to the exile of Bishop John Chrysostom in 403 (John had disapproved of Isaac's refusal to remain inside the monastery's walls).[7] The second immigrant was Jonah, a former soldier from Armenia who lived as an anchorite with a group of disciples in the Thracian town of Halmyrissos (possibly Salmydesseus, on the Black Sea some sixty miles northwest of Constantinople and the Bosporus, near modern Kıyıköy). Nothing is known about him beyond the sparse details contained in the *Life of Hypatius*. And the third immigrant was,

---

[4] For the Council of Gangra's having occurred in 358, putting it closer to the anti-homoiousian Council of Constantinople in 360, see Marta Przyszychowska, "The Date of the Council of Gangra Reconsidered (358)," *Journal of Early Christian Studies* 30 (2022): 223–43. For reports of Macedonius's violent zeal, see Sozomen, *Ecclesiastical History* 4.2.1–4.

[5] See Peter Hatlie, *The Monks and Monasteries of Constantinople, ca. 350–850* (Cambridge: Cambridge University Press, 2007), 64–65.

[6] Theodoret, *Ecclesiastical History* 4.35(34).1; Sozomen, *Ecclesiastical History* 6.40.1–2.

[7] See Peter Hatlie, "The Encomium of Ss. Isakos and Dalmatos by Michael the Monk (BHG3 956d): Text, Translation and Notes," in *EUKOSMIA. Studi miscellanei per il 75° d. Vincenzo Poggi S.J.*, ed. V. Ruggieri and L. Pieralli (Soveria Mannelli [Catanzaro]: Rubbettino, 2003), 275–311; also Sozomen, *Ecclesiastical History* 8.9.4, 8.19.3.

of course, Hypatius, who came from Phrygia and established connections with both Jonah and Isaac (2.8–12, 11.2) before setting up his own monastery at the Rufinianae across the Bosporus from Constantinople. While the widespread ascetic fervor in the imperial capital region may not have compared to that of the Egyptian desert or the Syrian countryside, there was clearly some enthusiasm to place monastic life near the political center of gravity, and it is the *Life of Hypatius* that offers us the earliest window through which we might catch a glimpse of this activity.

The text was written by someone identified as Callinicus, but our view of the author is hazy at best. He numbers himself among Hypatius's disciples and writes himself into the narrative at several points by noting that he was present to observe one of Hypatius's miracles or to receive one of his teachings (Prol.15, 4.5, 16.5, 17.6, 23.1, 23.3, 25.1, 27.6, 34.1, 35.13, 38.2), and that he was present at Hypatius's death (51.1), just before which Hypatius explicitly appointed his successor (51.6). Was the author, in an act of monastic humility, suggesting that he himself had been appointed as Hypatius's successor, or was he simply a later admirer who declined to name Hypatius's successor? Regardless, we do know that he chose to remain anonymous. We only learn the name from a later editor, who, in an opening dedication for a certain Eutyches, describes the author as "someone named Callinicus, one of his disciples" (Ded.2). The editor himself says that, during a visit to the Rufinianae monastery, he received the text directly from the third abbot and felt compelled to make a few syntactical corrections because of the Syrian dialect of Greek in which the text was composed. That is, like the three monastic protagonists of his work (Hypatius, Jonah, and Isaac), Callinicus was also an immigrant to Bithynia. It is possible that Callinicus was the second abbot— successor to Hypatius, predecessor to the unnamed third abbot— but, had Callinicus been the second abbot (something the third abbot and, by extension, the editor would have surely known), we might expect the editor to have identified Callinicus as such rather than as one of Hypatius's mere disciples.

Another possibility emerges if we consider the question of when the text was composed. Gerard Bartelink, who made the text's critical edition, represents the consensus view in claiming that the text was written soon after Hypatius's death, which evidence within the *Life* suggests occurred in 446. Because the author notes that Thrace had not yet recovered from the Hunnic invasion of January 447 (52.4–8), which Hypatius predicted before his death (52.1–3), and because there is no mention of the Council of Chalcedon in 451, Bartelink dates the text to 447–450.[8] Previously, Hans-Georg Beck had voiced his support for a sixth-century date,[9] and recently Timothy D. Barnes noted that the anachronistic portrayal of the Olympic games being banned in the time of Hypatius (33.1), as well as a possibly anachronistic use of the Greek *illoustrios* to translate the Latin *illustris* as a rank and title, supports a sixth-century dating for the text.[10] If that is correct, then obviously it would be impossible for the author to have known Hypatius personally. Yet late antique hagiographies have a well-earned reputation for fully inventing the social, cultural, legal, and religious reality in which their saints live, and so perhaps we should avoid investing too much stock in any perceived historical inaccuracies. Moreover, Barnes himself notes that there is one fifth-century example of the Greek *illoustrios* translating the Latin *illustris* (the minutes of the Council of Ephesus in 431); would it be too much to allow for a second example in the *Life of Hypatius*? We might be tempted to look at the manuscripts to shed light on the date and authorship, and yet there is little to be learned. Three primary manuscripts and one palimpsest that Bartelink describes as nearly illegible serve as the bases for the *Life of Hypatius*. The three manuscripts—

---

[8] G. J. M. Bartelink, *Callinicos: Vie d'Hypatios*, Sources chrétiennes 177 (Paris: Éditions du Cerf, 1971), 11–12.

[9] Hans-Georg Beck, *Kirche und theologische Literatur im byzantinischen Reich*, Byzantinisches Handbuch im Rahmen des Handbuchs der Altertumswissenschaft 2.1 (Munich: C. H. Beck'sche Verlagsbuchhandlung, 1959), 404.

[10] Timothy D. Barnes, *Early Christian Hagiography and Roman History*, 2nd rev. ed. (Tübingen: Mohr Siebeck, 2016), 246–48.

Vaticanus graecus 1667 (10th cent.), *Parisinus graecus* 1488 (11th cent.), and *Athoniensis Philotheou* 8 (11th cent.)—each contain a *menologion*, that is, an ecclesiastical calendar that presents a hagiographical narrative of a saint according to the saint's feast day (in Hypatius's case, the text appears on June 17 according to *Athoniensis Philotheou* 8, and June 30 according to *Vaticanus graecus* 1667). None contains scholia or marginalia that comment on the author's identity. The same is true of the earliest scholarly editions of the text, including the Bollandists' *Acta Sanctorum*, which says little about the author or date of composition.[11] In the absence of any additional evidence supporting a sixth-century date, we must tentatively take the text at its word, that Callinicus, a disciple of Hypatius and possibly the second abbot of the Rufinianae, composed the hagiographical narrative not long after the saint's death, with the acknowledgment that any firm assertion of date or authorship is tenuous at best.

Our knowledge of Hypatius's monastery is more secure. The renowned Bollandist scholar Hippolyte Delehaye noted that the Rufinianae was one of the most important monasteries in the Constantinopolitan milieu.[12] The property existed because of the beneficence of Flavius Rufinus, a well-documented imperial official active during the reign of Theodosius I (379–395).[13] As Master of Offices (388–392), Consul Posterior (392), and Praetorian Prefect of the East (392–395), he was a notorious political operator; he accused one of his rivals of corruption, orchestrated his execution, and then took his illustrious position. So trusted an advisor and

---

[11] See *Acta Sanctorum Junii, Tomus III*: De S. Hypatii Abb. In Rufinianis (Antwerp, 1701), 303–49.

[12] Hippolyte Delehaye, "Byzantine Monasticism," in *Byzantium: An Introduction to East Roman Civilization*, ed. Norman H. Baynes and H. St. L. B. Moss (Oxford: Clarendon Press, 1948), 144.

[13] See A. H. M. Jones, J. R. Martindale, and J. Morris, ed., *The Prosopography of the Later Roman Empire, Volume I: A.D. 260–395* (Cambridge: Cambridge University Press, 1971), 778–81, Flavius Rufinus 18, with many relevant citations of primary sources.

confidant was he to Emperor Theodosius I that Theodosius appointed Rufinus as guardian to his son and heir Arcadius. Rufinus was known to be a pious Christian, as is shown by the moralizing, anti-pagan, and anti-heretical laws that he received and enforced.[14] Arcadius's accession to the imperial throne gave Rufinus extensive power, but changes in the political landscape after Theodosius's death, and Rufinus's failure to arrange his daughter's marriage to the young emperor, made his power short-lived and unstable. Indeed, his western counterpart and rival Stilicho successfully orchestrated his assassination in late 395.

Before his death, Rufinus funded a major construction project that came to completion in 392 at a place known as the Oak (in Greek, *Drys*).[15] The location is perhaps the modern Caddebostan neighborhood of Kadıköy, just a few miles east of late antique Chalcedon and across the Bosporus from Constantinople.[16] Rufinus's ecclesiastical compound (hence the "Rufinianae") consisted of three primary structures: a palace, an apostolic church built in honor of Peter and Paul, and a monastery to house imported Egyptian monks, who also performed the church's clerical obligations.[17] These Egyptian monks were the "Tall Brothers" (Ammonius, Dioscorus, Eusebius, and Euthymius), who had been driven from the Nitrian desert by Bishop Theophilus of Alexandria in the early stages of the Origenist Controversy.[18] Their protection, guaranteed by Bishop John Chrysostom, was short-lived, for the Rufinianae became the site for the Synod of the Oak, which Theophilus attended and where he issued accusations that led to

---

[14] See *Theodosian Code* 9.7.7–8, 16.5.25–26, 16.10.12–13.

[15] For the location, see *Barrington Atlas of the Greek and Roman World*, ed. Richard J. A. Talbert (Princeton: Princeton University Press, 2000), 797, and map 53 of the Bosporus.

[16] See Raymond Janin, *Les églises et les monastères des grands centres byzantins (Bithynie, Hellespont, Latros, Galèsios, Trébizonde, Athènes, Thessalonique)* (Paris: Institut Français d'Études Byzantines, 1975), 38–40.

[17] Sozomen, *Ecclesiastical History* 8.17.3.

[18] See Socrates, *Ecclesiastical History* 6.7.1–29.

the downfall and exile of Chrysostom in 403.[19] The buildings of the compound were quite impressive, according to later reports: Palladius, the devoted follower and biographer of John Chrysostom, refers to the place as "Rufinus's suburb," while the Latin poet Claudian mocks Rufinus and the estate (Claudian was, after all, a partisan for Rufinus's rival, Stilicho) but gives a sense for the structures' magnitude by comparing them to the Egyptian pyramids and noting that the mausoleum that Rufinus built for himself "outdid all other temples, as an ornament for his departed spirit."[20] Unfortunately, nothing remains of the physical structure for archaeologists to assess, but it is notable that several different writers—of different genres, of different religious commitments, in different languages, and in different locations—attest to the existence of the site.

Hypatius established his monastic community at the Rufinianae accidentally. He and his colleagues Timothy and Moschius left the Constantinopolitan suburbs where they had been residing in search of a mountain or cave, somewhere more rugged where they could practice asceticism. They passed through Chalcedon and, in 406 (dated using evidence internal to the *Life*), stumbled upon the Rufinianae. The buildings to which the *Life* refers were the monastery and the apostolic church. But when Hypatius, Timothy, and Moschius arrived, the whole place had been fully abandoned. The structure contained "both a courtyard surrounded by cells and a chapel that had gone long neglected," with a room designed for quiet work (8.11), but before they arrived, "the structure was large and deserted, causing it to fill with snow during the winter" (8.13). The ascetic trio moved in, cleaned it up (a task that included exorcising a demon that had attached to the place), and eventually populated the monastery with roughly fifty monks (18.2). At some

---

[19] For a helpful summary of the event, see Henry Chadwick, *The Church in Ancient Society* (Oxford: Oxford University Press, 2001), 494–98.

[20] Claudian, *Against Rufinus* 2:446–49 (trans. Neil W. Bernstein, *The Complete Works of Claudian* [London and New York: Routledge, 2023], 118).

point, possibly after December 434, they received financial support from the imperial official Urbicius to renovate and expand the facility (12.13).[21]

While Callinicus describes the location of the monastery as "quite remote" (8.7), it could not have been too far from the apostolic church, Rufinus's palace, or the adjacent villages and settlements, as the *Life* describes the frequent interactions Hypatius has with nearby clergy members, imperial officials, villagers, soldiers, and wealthy estate holders, and indeed the site was known and used by emperors as a convenient meeting spot or as a benefice to high-ranking officials. In addition to the Synod of the Oak in 403, Emperor Theodosius II convened delegates there in September 431 from rival factions of bishops—those loyal to Cyril of Alexandria and those loyal to Nestorius of Constantinople—for hearings in the aftermath of the shambolic Council of Ephesus held earlier that summer.[22] So embedded within this suburban community was the monastery that some later texts referred to the suburb as a whole (structures, villages, estates) as a single unit; Procopius's *History of the Wars* mentions the Rufinianae as the private possession of Justinian's general Belisarius,[23] and Cyril of Scythopolis's *Life of Saba* notes that its ascetic protagonist resided briefly in the "the suburb of Rufinus tenanted by Demostratus."[24] Other texts, such as the fifth-century *Life of Auxentius*, mention

---

[21] Urbicius too is well documented. See J. R. Martindale, *The Prosopography of the Later Roman Empire, Volume II: A.D. 395–527* (Cambridge: Cambridge University Press, 1980), 1188–90, Urbicius 1, with many relevant citations of primary sources.

[22] See Kenneth Holum, *Theodosian Empresses: Women and Imperial Dominion in Late Antiquity*, Transformation of the Classical Heritage 3 (Berkeley: University of California Press, 1982), 171–72, with references.

[23] Procopius, *History of the Wars* 1.25.23–24.

[24] See Cyril, *Life of Saba*, ed. E. Schwartz, *Kyrillos von Skythopolis*, Texte und Untersuchungen 49.2 (Leipzig: Hinrichs, 1939), 145: *tò proástion Rouphínou toû katà Dēmóstraton*. On the translation of *katá* as "tenanted by," see Alan Cameron, "Cyril of Scythopolis, V. Sabae 53: A Note on κατά in Late Greek," *Glotta* 56 (1978): 88.

the Rufinianae in apposition to the monastery of blessed Hypatius, as does the Constantinopolitan *Synaxarion*.[25] At some point, the Rufinianae gained additional honor by becoming a commemoration site for Saints Sergius and Bacchus, but by 1236 the monastery sank into financial ruin and, unable to support itself, was absorbed into another monastic community.[26]

The *Life of Hypatius*, which narrates the activity of the monastery's founder and foundation, belongs to the genre, or perhaps discursive mode,[27] of monastic hagiography, a literary family that emerged in the fourth century and flourished in the fifth and sixth centuries. This genre centers around the subject of a saint whose unflinching holiness is made manifest to all by a strict ascetic regimen, a preternatural ability to teach and attract disciples, an innate understanding of theological orthodoxy, an ability to work miracles, and a talent for waging spiritual warfare against demons and Satan as well as heretics, pagans, and Jews. Collectively, the authors of monastic hagiographies utilize stock characters, generic conventions, and standard narrative structures as they depict and memorialize the sanctity of their protagonist.[28] The textual result is quite idealistic: there is no question regarding the truth of the saint's teachings or the purity of the saint's intentions, and the saint's relationships with disciples are always irreproachable and the miracles incontrovertible. The very point of this discursive mode is to identify a locus of divine power and to depict it in various contexts (during youth, in instruction, amidst various social interactions, and often at death).

---

[25] *Life of Saint Auxentius*, 38–39; *Synaxarium of the Constantinopolitan Church*, June 17.2, ed. Hippolyte Delehaye (Brussels: Société des Bollandistes, 1902), 754.

[26] For a full and detailed overview, see Jules Pargoire, "Rufinianes," *Byzantinische Zeitschrift* 8 (1899): 429–77.

[27] See Marc van Uytfanghe, "L'hagiographie: un 'genre' chrétien ou antique tardif?," *Analecta Bollandiana* 111 (1993): 135–88, esp. 147–49.

[28] On the generic conventions of hagiography, see Marc van Uytfanghe, "L'origine et les ingredients du discours hagiographique," *Sacris Erudiri* 50 (2011): 35–70.

The predictable and derivative, not to mention fantastical, character of monastic hagiographies has prompted some historians to criticize them. With characteristic polemic, Edward Gibbon, the eighteenth-century historian of Rome's decline and fall, identified them as particularly noxious: "These extravagant tales, which display the fiction, without the genius, of poetry, have seriously affected the reason, the faith, and the morals, of the Christians. Their credulity debased and vitiated the faculties of the mind; they corrupted the evidence of history; and superstition gradually extinguished the hostile light of philosophy and science."[29] Yet hagiographers knew what they were doing—the repetition and preposterousness was often an important component of the literary project—and were themselves aware of "the dangers of homogenized characterization."[30] Such awareness freed some authors to play with, even subvert, the expectations readers might have brought to the text. More than that, though, brushing off monastic hagiographies as uninteresting misses what makes them valuable to the historian of late antique Christianity: hagiographers inscribed stories and teachings of monastic heroes in the service of narrative world-building. *Lives* offered writers a literary venue in which they could construct a unified vision for the best way to live the monastic life, the best way to form and maintain a monastic community, the ethical standards to which monks should aspire and the lifestyles that they should spurn, the orthodoxy to which monks should cleave, and the best way to conduct social relationships with clergy members, government officials, and the broader world

---

[29] Edward Gibbon, *The History of the Decline and Fall of the Roman Empire, Volume II: A.D. 476–1461* (New York: The Modern Library, 1932), 17 (chap. 37).

[30] James Corke-Webster and Christa Grey, "Introduction," in *The Hagiographical Experiment: Developing Discourses of Sainthood* (Leiden: Brill, 2020), 11. For the conventional portraits of saints in hagiographies, see Robert Browning, "The 'Low Level' Saint's Life in the Early Byzantine World," in *The Byzantine Saint*, ed. Sergei Hackel (Crestwood, NY: Saint Vladimir's Seminary Press, 2001), 117–27.

around. In short, these texts advertise, in an almost propagandistic way, a vision for how the Christian life can best be lived.[31]

It was in the fourth century, with the increasing imperialization of Christianity, that monastic hagiographies emerged, lagging just behind the broader rise of monasticism itself. Perhaps the earliest and certainly the most popular representative is Athanasius of Alexandria's *Life of Antony*, written sometime around 360 and swiftly translated into Latin (twice) and Syriac before being eventually translated into Coptic and Old Church Slavonic.[32] Its impact was enormous—traceable in writers such as Gregory of Nazianzus (ca. 330–390), Jerome of Stridon (ca. 345–420), Augustine of Hippo (354–430), Paulinus of Milan (d. after 412), Sulpicius Severus (ca. 363–420), Palladius of Hellenopolis (ca. 363–430), and even Callinicus[33]—and its publication paved the way for a slew of other monastic hagiographies across the Roman world. In Egypt, several versions (Greek and Coptic) of the *Life of Pachomius* circulated before the end of the late fourth century, while the *Life of Aphu* probably appeared in the mid-fifth century.[34] Egypt was also, it seems, the birthplace of collections of monastic hagiographies like the anonymous *History of the Monks of Egypt*, which Rufinus of

---

[31] For hagiographical literature from late antiquity and the Byzantine period, see the excellent collection of topical and thematic essays in Stephanos Efthymiadis, ed., *The Ashgate Research Companion to Byzantine Hagiography, Volume I: Periods and Places*, Ashgate Research Companions (London and New York: Routledge, 2011); and Stephanos Efthymiadis, ed., *The Ashgate Research Companion to Byzantine Hagiography, Volume II: Genres and Contexts*, Ashgate Research Companions (London and New York: Routledge, 2014).

[32] On the historical context and theological vision that informed Athanasius's composition of the Life of Antony, see David Brakke, *Athanasius and the Politics of Asceticism*, Oxford Early Christian Studies (Oxford: Oxford University Press, 1992), 201–65.

[33] For the pre-modern translations and a fuller list of those influenced by the text, see G. J. M. Bartelink, ed. and trans., *Athanase d'Alexandrie. Vie d'Antoine*, Sources chrétiennes 400 (Paris: Éditions du Cerf, 1994), 68–70, 97–101.

[34] See Armand Veilleux, *Pachomian Koinonia, Volume One: The Life of Saint Pachomius and His Disciples*, Cistercian Studies 45 (Kalamazoo, MI: Cistercian Publications, 1980), 1–21; also *Life of Aphu* (E. Revillout, ed., "La vie du bienheureux Aphou," *Revue Égyptologique* 3 [1883]: 28–33).

Aquileia translated into Latin in 403.[35] In Cappadocia Gregory of Nazianzus and Gregory of Nyssa (ca. 335–395) composed quasi-monastic hagiographies for their respective sisters, Gorgonia and Macrina,[36] and in Galatia Palladius composed his *Lausiac History* (ca. 420), another hagiographical collection, which overlapped in some monastic characters with the *History of the Monks of Egypt*.[37] At Chalcis and then Bethlehem, Jerome wrote monastic hagiographies for Paul (376) as well as Malchus (388) and Hilarion (pre-392).[38] In Gaul, Sulpicius Severus composed the *Life of Martin* (ca. 396).[39] In Edessa, Ephrem composed, in his native Syriac, *madrashe* on the monks Julian Saba and Abraham of Qidun; the latter, along with his niece Maria, was the subject of a late fourth- or early fifth-century monastic hagiography.[40] Indeed, the later fifth century would see a proliferation of monastic hagiographies,

[35] *History of the Monks of Egypt*, ed. and trans. A.-J. Festugière, *Historia monachorum in Aegypto: Édition critique du texte grec*, Subsidia Hagiographica 34 (Brussels: Société de Bollandistes, 1961). For the date, see Andrew Cain, *The Greek* Historia Monachorum in Aegypto: *Monastic Hagiography in the Late Fourth Century*, Oxford Early Christian Studies (Oxford: Oxford University Press, 2016), 39–40.

[36] Gregory of Nazianzus, *Oration* 8 (PG 35:789–817); Gregory of Nyssa, *Life of Macrina*, ed. and trans. Pierre Maraval, *Grégoire de Nysse: Vie de sainte Macrine*, Sources chrétiennes 178 (Paris: Éditions du Cerf, 1971).

[37] Palladius of Helenopolis, *Lausiac History*, ed. G. J. M. Bartelink, *Palladio. La storia lausica*, Vite dei Santi 2 (n.p.: Lorenzo Valla, 1974).

[38] Jerome, *Life of Paul, Life of Malchus*, and *Life of Hilarion*, ed. Edgardo Morales, *Jérôme. Trois vies de moines (Paul, Malchus, Hilarion)*, Sources chrétiennes 508 (Paris: Éditions du Cerf, 2007). On Jerome's authorship of Paul, see Stefan Rebenich, "Inventing an Ascetic Hero: Jerome's *Life of Paul the Hermit*," in *Jerome of Stridon: His Life, Writings and Legacy* (London: Routledge, 2007), 13–16.

[39] Sulpicius Severus, *Life of Martin*, in *Sulpicius Severus' Vita Martini*, ed. and trans. Philip Burton (Oxford and New York: Oxford University Press, 2017).

[40] Ephrem, "Hymns of Abraham of Qidun and Julian of Saba," in Edmund Beck, *Des heiligen Ephraem des Syrers Hymnen auf Abraham Kidunaya und Julianos Saba*, ed. Edmund Beck, Corpus Scriptorum Christianorum Orientalium 322, Scriptores Syri 140 (Leuven: Peeters, 1972); "Acts of the Blessed Monk, Abraham of Qidun," in "Acta Beati Abrahae Kidunaiae Monachi," ed. T. J. Lamy, *Analecta Bollandiana* 10 (1891): 5–49.

including Theodoret's *Religious History* in Greek, Samuel's *Life of Barsauma* in Syriac, and Koriwn's *Life of Mashtotsʻ* in Armenian.[41] These, and more, comprise the torrent of monastic hagiographies to which Callinicus's *Life of Hypatius* belonged in the wake of the *Life of Antony*.

Indeed the *Life of Antony* may very well have inaugurated monastic hagiography as a new literary mode that memorialized and propagandized its subject, but it would be a mistake to regard Athanasius's work as taking place in a vacuum. The *Life of Antony* participated in a well-established tradition of life-writing during antiquity and late antiquity.[42] Athanasius's most immediate influence seems to have been Iamblichus's *On the Pythagorean Life* (more commonly known as the *Life of Pythagoras*), written sometime in the late third or early fourth centuries to train students how to live the philosophical lifestyle and how to pass along divine

---

[41] Theodoret, *Religious History*, ed. and trans. Pierre Canivet and Alice Leroy-Molinghen, *Histoire des moines de Syrie*, Sources chrétiennes 234 and 257 (Paris: Éditions du Cerf, 1977, 1979); Samuel, *The Life of the Syrian Saint Barsauma: Eulogy of a Hero of the Resistance to the Council of Chalcedon*, trans. Andrew Palmer, Transformation of the Classical Heritage 61 (Oakland: University of California Press, 2020); Koriwn, *The Life of Mashtotsʻ By His Disciple Koriwn*, ed. and trans. Abraham Terian, Oxford Early Christian Texts (Oxford: Oxford University Press, 2022).

[42] For an overview of the thorny debates about the biographical genre's taxonomy of features and conventions, see Koen de Temmerman, "Writing (about) Ancient Lives: Scholarship, Definitions, and Concepts," in *The Oxford Handbook of Ancient Biography* (Oxford: Oxford University Press, 2020), 7–12. For a rejection of genre and an embrace of the "biographic" in a multiplicity of literary, social, political, and religious contexts, see Simon Swain, "Biography and Biographic in the Literature of the Roman Empire," in *Portraits: Biographical Representation in the Greek and Latin Literature of the Roman Empire* (Oxford: Clarendon Press, 1997), 1–37. However fuzzy the category of "lives" or biographies might appear to modern scholars, ancient writers seemed to possess some idea of what a biography was and how it differed from other literary modes; see Sean A. Adams, "What are *Bioi*/Vitae? Generic Self-Consciousness in Ancient Biography," in *Oxford Handbook of Ancient Biography* (Oxford: Oxford University Press, 2020), 19–22.

wisdom.[43] Iamblichus's framework, purpose, concepts, and topics offered Athanasius a model of life-writing that he could apply and adapt to Antony.[44] Of course, *On the Pythagorean Life* itself participates in a broader literary family that includes philosophical, political, and spiritual life-writing, biographical anthologies, encomia, panegyric, and eulogies, of which there are too many examples to list.[45] As early as the late first and second centuries, Christians began to utilize the biographical tradition to lionize their heroes, writing gospels for the life of Jesus, *acta* for the lives of apostles, legends for the life of Jesus' mother Mary, *passiones* for the exploits of martyrs, and eventually hagiographies for saints, church fathers, and of course ascetics like Hypatius. Averil Cameron's comment about the importance of narrative literature to early Christians remains spot on: "Christianity was a religion with a story. Indeed, it possessed several different kinds of stories. But two were preeminent: *Lives*, biographies of divine or holy personages; and *Acts*, records of their doings, and often their deaths. Narrative is at their very heart; for whatever view one takes of the evolution of the Gospels, the remembered events and sayings from the life of Jesus were in fact strung together in a narrative

[43] See Iamblichus, *On the Pythagorean Life*, in *Iamblichi De vita Pythagorica liber*, ed. Ulrich Klein and Ludwig Deubner, Bibliotheca scriptorum Graecorum et Romanorum Teubneriana (Stuttgart: Teubner, 1975).

[44] See Samuel Rubenson, "Antony and Pythagoras: A Reappraisal of the Appropriation of Classical Biography in Athanasius' *Vita Antonii*," in *Beyond Reception: Mutual Influences between Antique Religion, Judaism, and Early Christianity*, ed. David Brakke, Anders-Christian Jacobsen, and Jörg Ulrich (Frankfurt am Main: Peter Lang, 2006), 191–208.

[45] For the classic treatment of the origins of biographical writing, see Arnaldo Momigliano, *The Development of Greek Biography*, expanded ed. (Cambridge, MA: Harvard University Press, 1993); for the classic treatment of biographical writing in the Roman period, see Friedrich Leo, *Die griechisch römische Biographie nach ihrer litterarischen Form* (Leipzig: Teubner, 1901); see the helpful overview of Sean A. Adams, *The Genre of Acts and Collected Biography*, Society for New Testament Monograph Series 156 (Cambridge: Cambridge University Press, 2013), 68–115.

sequence and ever afterward provided both a literary and a moral pattern."[46]

The *Life of Hypatius* participated in this broad biographical tradition, but Gerard Bartelink has identified two texts that exerted special influence on Callinicus. First, Athanasius's *Life of Antony* provided a template for Callinicus's *Life of Hypatius*.[47] Indeed, Callinicus explicitly compares Hypatius to Antony near the text's conclusion: "And so Saint Hypatius did all things in line with our holy father Antony, even with respect to his sister. Just as [Antony] had one sister, so too did [Hypatius]. Yes, while he was going about in the flesh, Saint Hypatius used to say, 'Children, know that I regard our father Saint Antony as just after the holy apostles. He embraced me, he blessed me, and, after performing a prayer, he dismissed me'" (53.4–6). The testimony of the Life notwithstanding, there is no additional evidence that Hypatius ever encountered Antony face-to-face. At the level of general comparison, Hypatius, like Antony, performs intense asceticism, battles demons, refutes heretics, instructs his disciples, and encourages unceasing prayer, but many details reveal that Callinicus borrowed much from Athanasius. There are structural similarities: each text begins the narrative with information pertaining to homeland, education, and family (*Life of Antony* 1.1 // *Life of Hypatius* 1.1). There are similar family dynamics (each saint was eighteen and had a sister whom he left behind before taking up the ascetic life (*Life of Antony* 2.1 // *Life of Hypatius* 2.3[48] and *Life of Antony* 2.1, 4 // *Life of Hypatius* 1.8, 53.4). Each took up the ascetic life after listening to a reading from the Gospel of Matthew (*Life of Antony* 2.3 [Matthew 19:21] // *Life of Hypatius* 1.7 [Matthew 19:29]). Callinicus even uses some

---

[46] Averil Cameron, *Christianity and the Rhetoric of Empire: The Development of Christian Discourse*, Sather Classical Lectures 55 (Berkeley: University of California Press, 1991), 89.

[47] See Bartelink, *Callinicos*, 33–38. All the points of correspondence listed below were noticed by Bartelink.

[48] Although the *Life of Antony* notes that Antony was "around eighteen or twenty years old."

of the same Greek phrasing and constructions that Athanasius does, like calling Satan the "hater of good" (*ho misókalos*; *Life of Antony* 5.1 // *Life of Hypatius* 9.1) and deploying the unusual phrase "neighboring monasteries" (*synechê monastéria*; *Life of Antony* 3.2 // *Life of Hypatius* 11.1).[49]

Second, Callinicus drew on the so-called *Spiritual Homilies* of Pseudo-Macarius for a range of material.[50] This textual corpus comprises sermons, questions and answers, and letters, which collectively put forth a mystical program that guides "true Christians"

---

[49] Also, both saints attribute the ability to heal to God, while insisting that they are merely human beings (Athanasius, *Life of Antony* 48.2 // *Life of Hypatius* 9.8), as do some of the people they heal (Athanasius, *Life of Antony* 56.2 // *Life of Hypatius* 22.6); both present classical education and philosophical rhetoric as antithetical to the monastic life (Athanasius, *Life of Antony* 77.1–5 // *Life of Hypatius* 29.3); both make prophecies that prompt the author to ask how the saint could do so except through God's love (Athanasius, *Life of Antony* 86.5 // *Life of Hypatius* 52.9). Both authors praise their subjects for *toîs gàr páschousi synépaschen*, "suffering with those who suffer" (Athanasius, *Life of Antony* 56.1 // *Life of Hypatius* 12.3); both have their subjects teach, *mête deiliômen tàs phantasías*, "let us not be afraid of [the Devil's] mental images" (Athanasius, *Life of Antony* 24.7 // *Life of Hypatius* 24.103); and both encounter a demon after smelling a *pikrâs dysōdías*, "a pungent stench" (Athanasius, *Life of Antony* 63.1 // *Life of Hypatius* 43.1).

[50] See H. Berthold, ed., *Makarios/Symeon, Reden und Briefe: Die Sammlung I des Vaticanus Graecus 694 (B)*, Die griechischen christlichen Schriftsteller der ersten Jahrhunderte 55 and 56 (Berlin: Akademie-Verlag, 1973) [= Collection I]; H. Dorries, E. Klostermann, and M. Kroeger, eds., *Die 50 Geistlichen Homilien des Makarios*, Patristische Texte und Studien 4 (Berlin: De Gruyter 1964, repr. 2010) [= Collection II (Homilies 1–50)]; V. Desprez, ed., *Pseudo-Macaire: Oeuvres spirituelles 1: Homélies propres à la Collection III*, Sources chrétiennes 275 (Paris: Éditions du Cerf, 1980) [= Collection III]; R. Staats, ed., *Makarios-Symeon: Epistola Magna. Eine messalianische Monchsregel und ihre Umschrift in Gregors von Nyssa "De Instituto Christiano"* (Gottingen: Vandenhoeck & Ruprecht, 1984); trans. George A. Mahoney, *Pseudo-Macarius: The Fifty Spiritual Homilies and the Great Letter*, The Classics of Western Spirituality (Mahwah, NJ: Paulist Press, 1992). On the authorship, see Dom L. Villecourt, "La date et l'origine des 'Homélies Spirituelles' attribuées à Macaire," *Comptes rendus des sessions de l'Académie des Inscriptions et Belles-Lettres* 64, no. 3 (1920): 250–58.

along a path of divinizing the soul by allowing for the Holy Spirit to indwell the human heart. The vision outlined by Pseudo-Macarius is thoroughly affective, centered on the interior experience of the individual, encouraging the reader to transcend material reality by uniting body, soul, and spirit in pure prayer. The spirituality found here corresponds to that of the Messalian movement, a style of Christian ascetic devotion that leans on a robust anticlericalism to assert that the surest way to receive the Holy Spirit is through the practice of ritualized apostolic poverty, itinerancy, and constant prayer.[51]

That Callinicus would be sympathetic to the Messalians is not surprising, given the *Life*'s praise for Alexander the Sleepless (41.1–10), a figure associated with the Messalians and the subject of his own monastic hagiography.[52] In the Pseudo-Macariana, Callinicus found material that he could appropriate and place into the mouth of Hypatius himself during his instruction to disciples.[53] For instance, the gnomic utterance of Hypatius, "If I'm not set free today,

[51] On the elements of Syrian spirituality present within the Pseudo-Macariana, see Columba Stewart, OSB, *"Working the Earth of the Heart": The Messalian Controversy in History, Texts, and Language to AD 431*, Oxford Theological Monographs (Oxford: Clarendon Press, 1991), 70–95, 234–40; Daniel Caner, *Wandering, Begging Monks: Spiritual Authority and the Promotion of Monasticism in Late Antiquity*, Transformation of the Classical Heritage 33 (Berkeley: University of California Press, 2002), 83–125. On the impact the Pseudo-Macariana had on later writers in late antiquity, see Marcus Plested, *The Macarian Legacy: The Place of Macarius-Symeon in the Eastern Christian Tradition*, Oxford Theological Monographs (Oxford: Oxford University Press, 2004).

[52] *Life of Alexander the Sleepless*, ed. E. de Stroope, *La vie d'Alexandre d'Acémète*, Patrologia Orientalis 6 (Paris: Firmin-Didot, 1911); trans. Daniel Caner, *Wandering, Begging Monks*, 249–80.

[53] This paragraph repeats the argument of G. J. M. Bartelink, "Text Parallels between the Vita Hypatii of Callinicus and the Pseudo-Macariana," *Vigiliae Christianae* 22 (1968): 128–36. Several parallels can be found among the two: Pseudo-Macarius, *Spiritual Homily* 11.4 // *Life of Hypatius* 48.1; Pseudo-Macarius, *Spiritual Homily* 30.113–14 // *Life of Hypatius* 28.57; Pseudo-Macarius, *Spiritual Homily* 10.2 // *Life of Hypatius* Prol.8; Pseudo-Macarius, *Spiritual Homily* 6.6.3, 7.5.5, 26.83, and 27.185 // *Life of Hypatius* 24.87; Pseudo-Macarius, *Spiritual Homily* 40.100 // *Life of Hypatius* 24.14.

I will be set free tomorrow; if not within five years, then within ten," finds its origin in Pseudo-Macarius (*Spiritual Homily* 26.11 [PTS 4:210] // *Life of Hypatius* 5.3), as does the concern about the grace of God leaving a human being, albeit for different reasons (e.g., *Spiritual Homily* 27.20, 294 [PTS 4:229] // *Life of Hypatius* 24.87). Where exactly Callinicus found these writings is uncertain, but it may very well have been in Syria—like the Pseudo-Macariana (and Alexander), Callinicus had a Syrian background (at least according to the editor of *Life of Hypatius*, who appears in the text's opening dedication).

It is one thing to delineate the literary context in which Callinicus wrote the *Life of Hypatius* and the textual influences from which he drew, but it is another to identify the author's motivation for writing in the first place. Fortunately, the *Life of Hypatius* contains two clues. The first emerges early, in the text's prologue, when Callinicus calls on readers to imitate the saints so that they may "be identified as co-heirs in eternal life" and then quotes Hypatius's exhortation to his disciples, "Children, if I were a smith or a carpenter, wouldn't you imitate me to learn the craft? So too now, become like me; learn fear of the Lord and how God is pleased" (Prol.6, 9).

The second clue presents itself in the episode of an unnamed scholasticus.[54] After being baptized by Hypatius, the man felt intense compunction and renounced the world, and requested that the *Life of Hypatius* be written in order to facilitate his imitation of the saint (35.16). Here Callinicus relates a story that explains the precise origins of the text. Perhaps Callinicus was himself the unnamed scholasticus, or perhaps the unnamed scholasticus commissioned Callinicus to write the *Life*, but, either way, Callinicus's intent in writing is clear: he wanted to spur readers to emulate the piety that Hypatius demonstrated in the text. The text was to be a model that showed the monks of the Rufinianae how to put Hypatius's ascetic ideals, teachings, and attitude, as Callinicus presents them, into daily practice.

---

[54] See 1.1, with the note.

What did that piety look like? For Hypatius, the monastic life is one of enslavement. The author identifies both himself as a slave of Christ (Prol.2) and his saintly subject as a slave of God (e.g., 3.5, 12.12, 14.8, 22.9, 28.10, 28.36, 29.50). Callinicus also identifies Hypatius's ascetic associates, Jonah and Timothy, as slaves of God (3.10 and 8.1–2) and remarks that when some characters renounce the world to take up the monastic life, they too have become enslaved to God (3.7, 35.17, 43.19, 44.25). Callinicus also notes that the archimandrite Isaac, who established the first monastery in Constantinople, and John Chrysostom, the short-tenured bishop of Constantinople, praised the ascetic residents of the Rufinianae for being true slaves of God (11.2, 5). The frequency with which phrases like "slave of God," "enslaved to God," "slave of Christ," or "slave of the Lord" appear in the *Life of Hypatius* (more than ninety times!) points to the centrality of the concept: for Hypatius, Callinicus, and the monks at Rufinianae, living the monastic life amounted to being a dutiful and loyal slave to God. In his valedictory speech just before his death, Hypatius beseeches his disciples to "focus on being authentically enslaved to the Lord" (50.4). Living the monastic life is living a life of virtuous, godly enslavement.

Callinicus did not coin the phrase; after all, biblical texts, apocryphal acts, and martyrdom narratives all applied "slave of God" to, respectively, Israelite patriarchs, Jesus' apostles, and Christian martyrs—the spiritually elite who were especially devoted to or favored by God.[55] However, in it he found an enormously rich theological and existential metaphor that allowed him to articulate a vision of the monastic project and the human condition writ large. We find this in the text's longest paraenetic discourse (24.1–104).

---

[55] See Athanasius, *Life of Antony* 18.1, 52.3, 85.5, for the sparing use of the phrase for Antony and the monastic life. Of the pre-monastic examples, see 2 Esdr 20:30 (LXX) and Rev 15:3, both of which refer to Moses as a "slave of God." The apostle John refers to himself as "a slave of the only God" in *Acts of John* 38, ed. Eric Junod and Jean-Daniel Kaestli, *Acta Iohannis: Praefatio–Textus*, Corpus Christianorum, Series Apocryphorum 1 (Turnhout: Brepols, 1983), 219.

Here Hypatius teaches that regardless of birth, nobility, rank, gender, race, ethnic group, or socioeconomic status, every human being shares the common lot of enslavement, which originates in the undeniable fact of human embodiment. Bodies render human beings as slaves to sin, temptation, disturbance, war, hardship, affliction, and, in a word, the world (24.51). By contrast, bodiless angels do not experience such things (24.40). To be a slave to the world is to yearn for physical and material comfort, for career security, marriage, and family, and for luxury in food and clothing; it is to be preoccupied with business, to be anxious about trends and fashions, to lust for money and possessions. All these things are "poisons" used by the Devil to distract human beings from focusing on God (24.16–17) and to cast a darkness over the human soul (24.19).

Yet the situation can be escaped by reorienting one's slavish existence and taking on a new Master. The slave of God realizes the vanity of worldly things, withdraws from them, and renounces all concerns "except for how to please God" (24.10). The slave of God builds a new life on the twin pillars of love for God and love for neighbor (24.3–4). In the ransom paid by Christ's incarnation (24.34), God has given monks a model for their own love of neighbors; in the salvation offered by Christ's incarnation, God "liberated us from enslavement to the world and its disturbances, and he brought us who live in tranquility to have no anxiety except how we may make a faultless presentation of our souls to the Lord" (24.44). Love for both God and neighbor generates virtues in God's slaves, such as "self-control, tranquility, endurance, possessionlessness, prudence, forbearance, and continuous lamentation for sin," virtues that will prompt the monks, like the angels, to glorify God with hymns of gratitude (24.36).

At the core of this new life of enslavement to God is an ascetic regimen that puts renunciation of the world into practice. Monks must cultivate self-control, a tool that "tames the body's passions, produces a pure mind, brings one to good knowledge, and sedates the vigor of youth" (24.63). While we might understand self-control as a state of bodily and emotional governance, Hypatius explains in his paraenetic discourse that it pertains specifically to food and diet. After all, he reasons, it was an overwhelming desire for diverse food that led both Adam to be expelled from the Garden of Eden and the Israelites to veer into idolatry (24.72–75, referring to Genesis 3:8–23, Exodus 16:3, and Numbers 11:5). The practice of self-control, from Hypatius's point of view, is the *sine qua non* of ascetic existence since it guides the monk to alimental simplicity. Indeed, Callinicus narrates with striking precision what the monk should eat and how often, and what other activities should accompany the minimalist diet:

> Saint Hypatius's diet was edible seeds, herbs, and a bit of bread, but in his old age, he partook of a bit of wine. He always ate at the end of the ninth hour, but often he postponed it, and during the forty-day fast he ate every other day while cloistering himself, singing, and praying Lauds, Terce, Sext, None, Vespers, Compline, and Matins, in accordance with the one who said, "Seven times a day I praised you for the judgments of your righteousness." He did this during each twenty-four-hour period, singing seven times one hundred psalms and one hundred prayers. Enacting this regimen until his death, he bequeathed it to his disciples, but even in his old age, he did not relent in the diet to which he held. For he always remained healthy, his body held strong, and his face was so fresh that [it looked] as if he partook of extravagant provisions. For truly, the saints partake of noble provisions when they derive enjoyment at the divine and spiritual table within the inner person. (26.1–5)

Hypatius adopts a vegan diet because this is what was laid out by his mentor Jonah, who avoided any meat or animal byproducts (3.6), but Hypatius also discusses it within the broader binary of enslavement to God versus enslavement to the world. The latter lures people to fleshly pleasure through epicurean decadence, while the former propels monks to simplicity of diet for the sake of sustenance. When paired with a regularized schedule of fasting and prayer, dietary simplicity further promotes the self-control that, in turn, facilitates subduing other passions, most notably sexual desire (5.1–2, 24.63).

For Hypatius, the root of monastic virtue is love of God and love of neighbor paired with the practice of self-control, but other virtues emerge as important components of the monastic life too. Humility features prominently as something that monks must generate in order to counteract the self-satisfaction, pride, or arrogance that may arise during ascetic training. Any personal achievement in self-control, Hypatius tells his listeners, comes through the grace of God, and self-satisfaction will almost certainly cause that grace to withdraw (24.82–93). More important, humility acts as the crucial counterbalance to ambition amidst the holy competition of monastic community. Within the monastic life, some ambition is healthy, even generative; early on, Hypatius himself engages his ascetic partner Timothy in a reverent rivalry that advances each man in virtue (8.10).

However, ascetic ambition left unchecked will almost inevitably become unanchored from humility, and so it might cause the monk's downfall. The long story of the arrogant monk Macarius illustrates this point (42.1–40). Macarius begins his renunciation with a strong devotion, and yet his singular focus on ascetic achievement brings him to ideas of grandeur, implanted by the Devil. So self-important does he become that eventually he lashes out at Hypatius and ends up dying as an excommunicant from the Rufinianae. As "an unbreakable wall and the crown of all the virtues" (24.90), humility proves just as important as self-control to the life of the monk, and it could be cultivated with the monk rooting himself in possessionlessness and a love for the poor: "The blessed one used to evince such possessionlessness and indifference to riches that he persuaded us by often saying, 'I have never had in my heart, "What have I ever acquired in this world?" but [only], "God appointed me a steward"'" (34.1). Hypatius seems to have rejected the very idea of private property and encouraged his disciples to separate themselves and their thoughts from luxury and material goods, a separation that opened them to progress in the life of the spirit and to live a lifestyle in alliance with the poor and destitute.

Indeed, service to the impoverished was a fundamental virtue at the Rufinianae monastery; even before Hypatius established the monastery, when he was dwelling with Jonah in Thrace, he asked for a commission "to minister exclusively to the afflicted" (4.2) on the basis of Matthew 25:34-36. The monks baked bread for the poor (18.1), distributed grain to the poor (20.1–2), and shared clothing with the poor (34.2). So devoted was Hypatius to alleviating the physical suffering and hardship of the impoverished people in the region that Callinicus could claim, perhaps not hyperbolically, that "no poor person ever left the monastery in need of anything. It is impossible to say how many wounds God treated through him" (22.4). For their part, the monks aimed simply to support themselves; whatever income they generated from making baskets and ropes or growing vegetables (8.11) went to fund the operation of the monastery, with leftover profits going to the poor.

Partnered with humility and possessionlessness was zeal. As expressed in this text, it is a value that might leave modern readers uneasy. It first appears in 30.1–12, where Hypatius's "zeal for God" is noted in apposition to a description of how he violently "purged many places in the Bithynian region of idolatrous error" by cutting down and burning trees used in non-Christian worship. Immediately on the heels of that sentence comes, first, an explicit call for Hypatius's disciples to erect virtue with violence (in Greek, *bia*) and, second, a pithy conclusion that reworks Matthew 11:12 to read, "For the kingdom of heaven belongs to the violent, and the violent take it by force" (30.12).[56] From Callinicus's perspective,

---

[56] *Biastôn gár estin hē basileía tôn ouranôn kaì biastaì harpázousin autén.* Matt 11:12 (NRSV) reads, "From the days of John the Baptist until now the kingdom of heaven has suffered violence, and the violent take it by force" (*apò dè tôn hēmrôn Iōánnou toû baptistoû héōs árti hē basileía tôn ouranôn biásetai kaì biastaì*

physical violence plays a constructive role in the monastic life, as illustrated in several episodes where Hypatius confronts practitioners of magic and divination, pagans, and demonically possessed individuals.

In one of these episodes, Hypatius causes his opponent, a practitioner of magic, to "recklessly devour his own tongue and hands"; the other monks protest in horror, but Hypatius allows the self-mastication to persist for a lengthy time as a punishment, presumably to put the overwhelming power of Christianity on display rather than to spur conversion, since the episode's conclusion has the man wandering off and eventually dying without becoming a true monk or even a Christian (28.23, 30). Another demonstration of violent zeal narrates how a certain Helpidius lived in a house with approximately forty men who sacrificed to idols, but he wanted to convert to Christianity and so abstained from offering sacrifice with the rest of the group. As a consequence, the other men thrashed him and expelled him from the house. After nursing Helpidius back to health and leading him to renounce the world, Hypatius demanded that the assailants repent and threatened, "If you don't, God's wrath will quickly overtake you!" The men refused, and within one year all of them were dead and the house itself "became vacant, as if no one ever lived there" at all (43.16–22). The death of the idolators seems, by the uncompromising logic and values of the text, unavoidable. Indeed, as Hypatius frames it later in a brief instruction that enlists a slew of martial, even belligerent, scriptural verses, being Christian requires participation in spiritual warfare to the point of blood (48.5). Violence and combat are as much a part of the monastic life as are humility, self-control, and love for the poor.

---

harpázousin autēn). This particular rendering of the biblical text seems to have originated in the Pseudo-Macariana (see, for instance, Pseudo-Macarius, *Spiritual Homily* 19.2 [PTS 4:183]). On the correspondence between the *Life of Hypatius* and the spiritual homilies of Pseudo-Macarius, see above, pp. 17–19.

The person charged with inculcating humility, possessionlessness, love for the poor, and zeal is, of course, Hypatius, the text's protagonist. The roots of his authority lie not only in the foundation of the Rufinianae monastery, but also in his role as spiritual father to all who revered piety and the ascetic life, be they the monks of the Rufinianae (10.8, 19.3), inhabitants of faraway cities like Rome and Alexandria (36.7), or even Emperor Theodosius II (37.2). The text portrays Hypatius as a vessel through which the Lord spoke (Prol.17) and acted (47.6-9), a man whose trustworthy teaching was based in Scripture (Prol.13), ascetic practice (4.1), and mystical revelations (10.4, 14.1-5). Hypatius, it seems, was destined to become an abbot and a teacher (2.6), but he frames his own leadership within the broader project of ascetic humility. Anytime pride or self-satisfaction appears in his thoughts, he calls himself back to humility by remembering that his own success was irreversibly tethered to that of his less experienced disciples (48.35–36).

Hypatius's role as abbot and teacher no doubt focused on the spiritual well-being of monks within the walls of the Rufinianae, but the *Life* makes it clear just how much the surrounding villages and towns also depended on him. People appreciated him, even to an extreme degree. Particularly haunting is the story Callinicus tells in which a child named Benjamin, who after having renounced the world alongside his father prayed for Hypatius because the saint had fallen ill: "Lord, because of the brothers and the needy, take me instead of the Abba!" Sure enough, the child died soon thereafter in an act of self-sacrifice to save Hypatius's life (18.5–6).

That Hypatius's leadership and piety proved advantageous to anyone near him—be they other monks, imperial officials, or villagers—signals how Callinicus's depiction of him fits the paradigm of the late antique holy man. More than fifty years ago, Peter Brown commented on the social role of the holy man in the eastern Roman Empire as someone who performed miracles and exorcisms, used curses to demonstrate divine power, spoke the truth frankly to powerful people, distributed blessings on God's behalf, and arbitrated quotidian disputes between supplicants. In the holy man, "the acute ambivalence of a Christian God was summed up in a manageable and approachable form."[57] Like a living relic, Hypatius possessed a sanctity that flowed out from his bodily presence, and so, naturally, the people in areas closest to him profited from his holy potency—the monks of Rufinianae and of nearby monasteries as well as the peasants in various unnamed Bithynian villages.

We might be tempted to assume that a holy man so close to the imperial capital would prove beneficial to its populace, and yet Constantinople barely figures in Callinicus's narrative.[58] Rather, Hypatius's power and authority extend to the rural population of laborers, fieldhands, farmers, and artisans—people who can most benefit from Hypatius's love for the poor. In the wake of Hunnic invasions, the saint advocates for the poor and destitute (6.1–4); in times of abundance, he distributes the grain harvest amongst the poor (20.1–2), and in times of famine, he miraculously feeds people (31.1–8); on multiple occasions he provides the poor with medical care (4.6–7, 22.1–6). He arbitrates disputes about marriage dowries (28.31–37). His miracles are the stuff of service—protection (38.6–9, 40.23–26, 46.1–5), healing (9.4–8, 15.1–2, 22.7–9, 38.3–5, 40.17–22, 44.34–36), and exorcism of both human beings (22.10–13, 22.14–29, 27.35–57, 40.1–4, 40.5–7, 40.8–16, 44.1–7, 44.20–23, 44.24–26) and livestock (22.21, 38.10, 38.14). Frequently, those very miracles prompt the recipients to renounce the world and join the monastery (40.27–36, 44.24–26). As a monastic hagiography, the *Life of Hypatius* tells the story of how the Rufinianae was established and

---

[57] Peter Brown, "The Rise and Function of the Holy Man," *Journal of Roman Studies* 61 (1971): 80–101, quoted at 97; see also the reconsiderations published more than twenty-five years later in Peter Brown, "The Rise and Function of the Holy Man, 1971–1997," *Journal of Early Christian Studies* 6 (1998): 353–76.

[58] The city is only mentioned four times—with reference to Isaac's monastery (1.6), to Jonah's visit to solicit resources from the wealthy for poverty relief in Thrace (5.4), and to Nestorius's being bishop (32.1, 39.1).

how the community came together, but it also depicts the social service that the saint and his community provided to Constantinople's suburban and exurban areas. To use the words of Callinicus, Hypatius was "like a physician given by God to this region, and, in the style of Job, he was a foot to the lame, an eye to the blind, a staff to the disabled, and a consolation to those who needed it" (44.37).[59]

Here as in other regions, an important part of the holy man's skill set was the detection and dispersal of demons, wherever they were—in places, structures, or individuals. Hypatius, like other monks from the fourth and fifth centuries, stood on the front line of a spiritual war.[60] Some monastic hagiographies inscribed a sense of drama into portrayals of the saint's conflict with the demonic. The *Life of Antony*, for instance, illustrates just how much a crucible Antony's conflict with the demons was; while not suspenseful, Athanasius's narrative conveys the physical and mental toll taken on the saint.[61] In the case of Hypatius, the theatricality comes not in the saint's harrowing experience but in the dominance that he exerts over his spiritual adversaries. The demons of the Thracian forest acknowledge his sanctity and flee at his mere presence, even though he himself is unaware of their presence (2.1–4). Even the demon (8.6)—or perhaps the Devil himself (9.1)—that inhabited the abandoned Rufinianae before the saint's arrival, who lingered in the form of a fiery ball that attacked the monks during prayer

---

[59] On the depiction of different socio-economic groups in the *Life of Hypatius*, see Jaclyn Maxwell, "Social Interactions in a Rural Monastery: Scholars, Peasants, Monks, and More in the *Life of Hypatius*," in *Motions of Late Antiquity: Essays on Religion, Politics, and Society in Honour of Peter Brown*, ed. Jamie Kreiner and Helmut Reimitz, Cultural Encounters in Late Antiquity and the Middle Ages 20 (Turnhout: Brepols, 2018), 89–106.

[60] See Cyril Mango, "Diabolus Byzantinus," *Dumbarton Oaks Papers* 46 (1992): 215–23, esp. 216–17. For a focused discussion of the role of demons in monastic writings and ascetic exercises, but in an Egyptian context, see David Brakke, *Demons and the Making of the Monk: Spiritual Combat in Early Christianity* (Cambridge, MA: Harvard University Press, 2006), 7–22.

[61] Athanasius, *Life of Antony* 5.1–6.3, 9.1–10.4.

(8.12) until the Lord finally drove it away (12.2), posed no real challenge to the saint.

The various exorcisms that pepper the *Life* more often than not offer Callinicus additional opportunities either to show Hypatius exercising holy power (40.5–7) or to have characters like suppliants or even the demons themselves provide an intra-narratival acknowledgment of his authority (44.1–7). Neither the demons nor the Devil ever really poses a threat to Hypatius and the monks of the Rufinianae, but their presence still advances the hagiographical narrative in meaningful ways. For instance, Hypatius and the Devil discuss whether it was even possible for the Devil to repent of his sins and be forgiven by God, an exchange that offered an indirect way for Hypatius (and the author Callinicus) to distance himself from any association with Origenism (15.3–8).[62] On another occasion, it is the Devil who saves Hypatius from a possibly fatal illness for the sole purpose of preserving him for a later showdown that never occurs (23.4).

On yet one further occasion, Hypatius expresses consternation that he cannot perform a healing miracle for someone, and so demons appear and reveal the man's unconfessed sins; Hypatius uses that information to confront the recipient of the miracle, extract a confession, and ultimately pass judgment: " 'When I asked you earlier, you failed to confess. Look, you've got three days left

---

[62] While Origen does not explicitly say so, the implications of his vision of the "great restoration" (*apokatástasis*) at the end of time was that the Devil and the demons would experience salvation and reincorporation into divine unity; see Origen, *On First Principles* 1.6.1, in *Origène. Traité des Principes. Tome I (Livres I et II)*, ed. Henri Crouzel and Manlio Simonetti, Sources chrétiennes 252 (Paris: Éditions du Cerf, 1978), 194–96, and *Against Celsus* 4.99, in *Origenes. Contra Celsum libri viii*, ed. M. Marcovich, Supplements to Vigiliae Christianae 54 (Leiden: Brill, 2001), 99. On the so-called Origenist controversy that emerged at the end of the fourth century and into the fifth, which had far-reaching effects including the exile of John Chrysostom, see Elizabeth A. Clark, *The Origenist Controversy: The Cultural Construction of an Early Christian Debate* (Princeton: Princeton University Press, 1992).

and then you will die. If you had proclaimed it and repented, we too would have implored God to forgive and heal you.' Eventually, the man lost hope and died three days later" (28.12–13). Is Hypatius determining and executing the penalty himself with this quasi-curse, or is he merely sealing the man's fate, already fixed by the man's attempt to conceal his sins? Whatever the interpretation, Hypatius's zeal rests on the sure foundation of righteous motivation, and so rather than drive the demons out of an otherwise innocent victim, the saint facilitates the elimination of the vessel—the man—that the demons possessed.

Hypatius's spiritual war against Satan and the demons informs the saint's successful opposition to the prefect Leontius's planned revival of the Olympic games at Chalcedon, an episode for which the *Life* is best known among scholars of late Roman history (33.1–16).[63] The effort stung Hypatius so sharply that he gathered a throng of twenty brothers (nearly half the monks living at the Rufinianae) and confronted Bishop Eulalius of Chalcedon with a choice: either the contests get canceled or Hypatius provokes the imperial officials to violence and thereby makes himself a martyr. When Leontius got word of Hypatius's plans, he backed down. Only at the end of the episode does Callinicus reveal the motivations behind Hypatius's resistance; he had heard that "the Olympic games were a wholly dreadful festival belonging to Satan, that it was completely filled with idol-mania, and that it would bring ruin and destruction to Christians" (33.16). It might be the case that the episode is entirely anachronistic,[64] but it allows Callinicus to embed Hypatius more fully within the cosmic conflict against Satan.

---

[63] See Juan Antonio Jiménez Sánchez, "The Monk Hypatius and the Olympic Games of Chalcedon," *Studia Patristica* 60 (2013): 39–45; for the episode as a portrayal of the broader debate in late antique Christian culture about who has the authority to use force (clergy members and imperial officials, or monks), see Peter Brown, "Christianization and Social Conflict," in *The Cambridge Ancient History. Volume XIII: The Late Empire, A.D. 337–425*, ed. Averil Cameron and Peter Garnsey (Cambridge: Cambridge University Press, 1998), 647.

[64] See Barnes, *Early Christian Hagiography*, 246–48.

Interestingly, it is not the prefect Leontius whom the *Life* targets as the foil to Hypatius here, but rather Bishop Eulalius, who confronts Hypatius by saying, "You would prefer to simply die even though no one is compelling us to sacrifice? You're a monk: sit down and shut up! This matter rests with me" (33.7). A few sentences later, Callinicus notes that "the bishop, even in other matters, often treated [Hypatius] with insolence and contempt" (33.9). The suggestion is implicit but damning: Eulalius is more a slave to the world than to God, which puts him in a spiritual position adjacent to Satan. Hypatius opposes not only the revival of the Olympic games because of their perceived Satanic influence but also the clergy member who willingly accommodates the prefect and who thinks that the monk's performance of zealous authority is out of line.

Here, again, readers might detect the influence of the Messalian movement, which, like Hypatius, kept a healthy suspicion of institutional clergy.[65] No doubt, certain members of the clergy come off well. Callinicus commends, for obvious reasons, the unnamed presbyter who encourages Hypatius to become a monk (2.8) and praises Bishop John Chrysostom for championing monks (11.5–7). Even the two protagonists of the *Life*—Jonah and Hypatius himself—join the presbyterate, albeit for their monastic communities (4.7, 13.2–3). On the other hand, Callinicus is aware that clerical office does not guarantee its occupant access to holiness. Early in the text, and perhaps as a way to describe the context that spurred Hypatius to the ascetic life, he notes that Phrygian churches, to the extent that there were any, were serviced by sluggish clergy during the saint's youth (1.4), and that drunken clergy members in Thrace disgusted Hypatius (2.10). Hypatius even boldly expels Nestorius from his church's diptychs, a declaration that the bishop of Constantinople's contemptible behavior and theology have rendered him unworthy of being a real bishop (32.14).

---

[65] See Caner, *Wandering, Begging Monks*, 150–57.

Callinicus's ire is most fearsomely reserved for clergy members who willingly accommodate worldly power and authority, like the sycophantic priests who do the bidding of the ex-consul Monaxius (21.8), and Eulalius, who not only accommodates the revival of the Olympic games but also chastises Hypatius for refusing to kowtow to Nestorius, the heretical bishop of Constantinople (33.12); when the holy Alexander the Sleepless shows up with his monks in Chalcedon, Eulalius chases them out and then threatens Hypatius with exile should he extend hospitality to them (41.5–10). As pleased as Callinicus is with the role that the Roman world and government played in promoting Christianity (24.47), he seems equally disappointed with the effect such growth had on the quality of clergy members. And yet, by presenting the drunk, sluggish, and accommodating clergy as foils to Hypatius, Callinicus only confirms the basic outlook of the *Life*: one can enslave oneself to God or to the world, but not both.

Callinicus stops short of stating that lukewarm clergy members have arrayed themselves with Satan, but he shows no hesitation in doing so with people who engage in non-Christian rituals and worship, particularly what the text frames as magic and idolatry. These categories of non-Christian religiosity consistently overlap in the text to such an extent that they are almost interchangeable—and all three are characterized as demonic or Satanic. Take, for instance, the episode of an Antiochene man who declares his intent to convert to Christianity but who, readers learn, wears a rag "from Artemis" around his waist that reeked of a "Satanic stench." Hypatius and his monks try to burn it but, rather than catching flame, the rag is transformed into a sphere, which Hypatius subsequently subjects to a ritualized performance of shame by smashing it, mixing it with dirt, and dumping it into the latrine. Afterward, Hypatius bids the man to retrieve his other "magical paraphernalia" to be destroyed too (43.1–8). On another occasion, Hypatius encounters Artemis herself as a "woman as tall as ten men" only after the text identifies her as a demon (45.3, 6). A particularly interesting episode involves Hypatius failing to heal a man with an ulcer on his thigh because the man had visited a witch before coming to the saint; during the night, the saint has a vision in which the witch consorts with the Devil and a host of demons, who eventually yield to Hypatius and allow the man to be properly healed (28.1–6).

The association between the demonic and the non-Christian informs Hypatius's zealous reaction to certain people he encounters. While on one occasion Urbicius, a patron of and financial contributor to the Rufinianae, sends his *domesticus* Alcimus to Hypatius for a healing because he has become desiccated from practicing magic (15.1–2)—thus soliciting a kind reaction from the saint—the episode of the forty idolators who lived together in a house (discussed above) and thrashed Helpidius for converting to Christianity concludes with their disintegration and death as well as the disappearance of the house itself (43.16–22). Hypatius forcefully imprisons another man, who acknowledges that his ability to divine the future stems from animal sacrifice at the "idol-temple," and Hypatius only releases him shortly before his death (43.9–15).

The threat of the magical and/or the demonic could threaten the sanctity of the monastery too, be it the Rufinianae or nearby communities. The man who intended to renounce the world and join Eumathius's monastery a few miles from the Rufinianae turns out to be a magician who cast demons against Hypatius, and so Hypatius punishes him with self-mastication (28.14–30). The long story of the monk Macarius, who joins the Rufinianae but whose monastic ambition leads to perdition, begins by noting that, before his renunciation, he "lived with magicians, because of which he developed a secret abnormality in his mind" (42.1). Toward such people, Hypatius evinces a merciless zeal that puts his own servitude to God on display.

For Callinicus and the monks of the Rufinianae with whom he dwells, Hypatius was a holy man whose enslavement to God manifested itself in a strict ascetic regimen, infallible instruction, and a role as an indefatigable defender of Christian cultural hegemony.

He was beholden to neither the imperial government, although he certainly respected the piety of rulers in the Theodosian dynasty (11.7, 37.1–3, 41.14), nor the clerical hierarchy in any way. Indeed, his antipathy for certain members of that hierarchy seems palpable at times, and he was unafraid to resist bishops whom he took to be deferring to anything Satanic. His uncompromising stance against idolatry, magic, heresy, and any accommodation to those things among the Christians was born out of the same zeal with which he monitored his own ascetic regimen and monastic leadership. Callinicus calls him a physician at one time (44.37) and a shepherd at another (2.6–7), two professional metaphors that show the qualities he understood Hypatius to possess: he was expected to protect and care for the body of Christ.

In short, Hypatius was a late antique holy man whose mere presence kept at bay Satan, demons, and other malign forces. He was a living Christian amulet, so to speak, an apotropaic saint whose value to the society around him was his ability to maintain the religious purity of the region by confrontation and then domination. Callinicus highlights this point in his description of the devastation to which the Hunnic tribes subjected Constantinople and its suburbs immediately after Hypatius died (52.1–9). More than that, though, Callinicus has inscribed Hypatius's lifestyle and conduct as a model for other monks to imitate. What distinguishes this hagiography from others in which the holy protagonist is violently zealous is its proactivity: Hypatius acts out a script designed to be reenacted time and again by readers, a script for piety that is neither gentle nor contemplative nor eremitic nor passive, but rough and sectarian and confrontational.[66] For the *Life of Hypatius*, the true Christian is the authentic monk, and the job of the authentic monk was to offer the peasants and laborers around him unmitigated and unobstructed access to holiness.

---

[66] See Bradley K. Storin, "Monastic Identity and Violence in Callinicus' *Vita Hypatii*," *Studia Patristica* 129 (2021): 155–66.

To conclude this brief introduction, it is worth reflecting on what modern readers can learn from the *Life of Hypatius*. The historical Hypatius lies behind several veils that impede modern readers from knowing him as he was in his own time. On the one hand, later monastic traditions in the Latin West and Greek East have relegated Hypatius to secondary status; after all, he does not number among the ranks of patristic luminaries like Athanasius of Alexandria, Gregory of Nazianzus, or Cyril of Alexandria, and he does not belong on the roster of ascetic celebrities like Antony of Egypt, Symeon Stylites, Macrina, or Melania the Elder. Neither the monastery of the Rufinianae nor the composition of Callinicus proved radically influential on later generations of Christians.

On the other hand, Hypatius lies behind the veil of generic conventionality. As was discussed above, monastic hagiographies so frequently utilize the tools of the genre—style, tropes, structure, narrative progression—that readers may wonder whether it is possible to use the *Life* to learn anything specific about the historical Hypatius. The consensus among scholars about the relationship between hagiography and history "as it happened" has been settled for a century or so. Hagiographies connect "imaginary events to an actual person" and locate "fantastical stories in a specific place";[67] they portray saints so that readers "can have access to their transcendent experience";[68] the purpose of hagiographical writings was "to communicate virtues to an audience through narrative."[69] Inasmuch as hagiographical texts comprise portraits of how things ought to be and not necessarily how things actually

[67] Hippolyte Delehaye, *Les légendes hagiographiques*, 2nd ed. (Brussels: Bureaux de la Société des Bollandistes, 1906), 9.

[68] Lynda L. Coon, *Sacred Fictions: Holy Women and Hagiography in Late Antiquity*, Middle Ages Series (Philadelphia: University of Pennsylvania Press, 1997), 9.

[69] Derek Krueger, *Writing as Holiness: The Practice of Holiness in the Early Christian East*, Divinations: Re-reading Late Ancient Religion (Philadelphia: University of Pennsylvania Press, 2004), 11.

were,[70] they present in narrative form the visions, values, and ideals of their respective authors, figures who bear the influence of their own social, cultural, political, and religious context and naturally hope that the narrative of sanctity resonates with the immediate reading audience. Very little aside from the basic facts of Hypatius's existence, his geographical location, and his establishment of the Rufinianae can be set down as historical, and so the conclusion is inescapable that readers learn more about Callinicus and his situation from the *Life of Hypatius* than they do about Hypatius himself.[71]

There is still much information to be gleaned from the *Life of Hypatius* even if that information cannot be related to the saint with certainty. If the scholarly consensus is correct about the *Life*'s being written shortly after Hypatius's death in the mid-fifth century by one of his disciples (or even by his successor as abbot), then we can still learn an immense amount of information about the writer and perhaps about the readers Callinicus had in mind. Out of the story of Hypatius's arrival at the Rufinianae emerges an origin story for the monastery's establishment; from the miracle stories and accounts of engagement with folks around the region emerges a portrait of how the community might have attracted new members; from the discussion of Urbicius and his material contribution to the monastery emerges an account of the structure's renovation and expansion.

More than that, though, the *Life of Hypatius* offers a precious witness to the perspectives, values, and attitudes of at least one

---

[70] Some monastic hagiographies have been known to invent out of whole cloth events that they present as otherwise historical. One exemplary text would be the *Life of Barsauma* (written perhaps a few decades after the *Life of Hypatius*), which identifies its saint as the direct cause of Emperor Marcian's death and as the indirect cause of the deaths of thousands of Jews gathered in Jerusalem. The same practice of narrative confabulation almost certainly applies to the miraculous occurrences, the long paraenetic discourses, and other parts of the *Life of Hypatius*.

[71] See also Thomas J. Heffernan, *Sacred Biography: Saints and Their Biographers in the Middle Ages* (Oxford: Oxford University Press, 1988), 38–71.

member of the early generation of monks in and around Constantinople. Here we find enthusiasm for imperial Christianity juxtaposed with a distrust for the worldliness of clergy members and an aggravated hostility toward traditional, local, and non-Christian worship practices. The expressions of warmth and positivity toward different monastic colleagues—the "Tall Brothers" from Egypt or the Messalian monastery of Alexander the Sleepless—betray a toleration, even an embrace, of monastic diversity. Indeed, perhaps this is why Hypatius's long paraenetic discourse focuses on the timeless and indisputable virtues that transcend context, virtues like humility, possessionlessness, care for the poor, self-control, and zealous commitment. What mattered was not someone's monastic style or identity, but rather which virtues they strove to cultivate.

Some subtle clues in the text also give us a sense for the monastery's participation, albeit mild, in the politically charged Christological controversies of the mid-fifth century. In fact, the convergence of a condemnation of Nestorius and praise for the Dalmatios monastery—the Constantinopolitan community inaugurated by Isaac but that later included the infamous Eutyches[72]—may signal support for the community's adherence to Miaphysite Christology. In sum, whatever frustration we may encounter at not being able to reach the "historical Hypatius" ought to be relieved by focusing on the integral role this text plays in offering modern readers a picture of the emergence of monasticism in the Constantinopolitan environs during the fifth century.

---

[72] For Eutyches at the Dalmatios monastery, see Michael Gaddis and Richard Price, *The Acts of the Council of Chalcedon*, Translated Texts for Historians 45 (Liverpool: Liverpool University Press, 2005), 1:25–30.

Note on Translation

This translation is based on the edition of G. J. M. Bartelink, *Callinicos. Vie d'Hypatios*, Sources chrétiennes 177 (Paris: Éditions du Cerf, 1971). The chapter numbers and section numbers follow Bartelink's division of the text.

The material inserted with brackets [ ] indicates an insertion implied but not explicit in the Greek. Its inclusion should offer clarity for the reader.

Also, Callinicus often incorporates Scripture into his own discourse, making biblical quotations and citations so fluid and flexible that they do not always correspond to the critical edition of the New Testament (NA[28]), even though it is clear which verse(s) he quotes. Consequently, I have chosen to translate all scriptural quotations myself.

The Life of Our Sacred Father, Hypatius of the Rufinianae

Dedication to Eutyches
by Unknown Editor

1. Blessed be God, who instructs humankind in knowledge,[1] who paradoxically reveals to infants what sages do not grasp.[2] 2. I know your enthusiasm, beloved brother Eutyches,[3] and your eagerness to associate with the saints, whether in person or through written accounts; I know too that you, amidst tremendous desires, are eager to nourish the inner person[4]—and I have found the *Life* of our most sacred father Hypatius, recorded and set out in narrative form by someone named Callinicus, one of his disciples. I have been eager to bring this much desired writing to your attention.

3. I know well that the *Life* omitted much about him and his sacred acts, some of which I have heard from the blessed Abba[5] himself and others of which I beheld with my own eyes,[6] [all of

---

[1] See Ps 93(94):10. N.B. The number in parentheses refers to the Masoretic text, which is the Hebrew text commonly used as the basis for most modern English translations; the number outside parentheses refers to the Septuagint, which is the Greek translation of the Jewish scriptures and the version used by Callinicus.

[2] See Matt 11:25; Luke 10:21.

[3] The identity of this Eutyches is unknown.

[4] 2 Cor 4:16.

[5] This is either Hypatius himself or the abbot of the Rufinianae contemporary to the unknown editor.

[6] This statement is unclear. Perhaps he means posthumous miracles like those attributed to Thecla at her shrine in Seleucia. Gilbert Dagron, *Vie et miracles de Sainte Thècle*, Subsidia Hagiographica 62 (Brussels: Société des Bollandistes, 1978).

which] deserve to be mentioned in a narrative. These I did not find included in the text. 4. And yet, less bothered by the shortcomings [of Callinicus's *Life*] than delighted by its contents, which comprises no small treasure for eager listeners and lovers of Christ, I put it together as if in a book[7] and sent it to Your Charity. 5. I found [the *Life*] by chance—or rather, by the design of Christ, the designer of all—when I was passing through the monastery at the Rufinianae, led by the third leader since the most blessed man had dwelled there. To him the disciple of the sacred elder had bequeathed these words, according to the grace given him, as he was returning to the Lord. It was he who composed these words just as they are placed here.[8]

6. For my part, I made some changes and standardized the apparent divergences from our customary pronunciation, [divergences] that can be attributed to the dialect of the Syrians and their corresponding aspiration.[9] For example, I changed the letter ē to ei, and the ō to an o, or vice versa, and made a few more small changes like this. This practice kept at bay any risk of my corrupting the text or subjecting the author to condemnation on the grounds that his tongue's idiosyncrasy might affect his readers' interpretation. 7. I thought it would be too bold to disturb the composition by adding or subtracting anything, supposing that readers would find his missteps into solecism, characteristic of a monk who begot and composed them in simplicity, sweeter than, even preferable to, my own forthright and graceless corrections, since I tend to think in a worldly wisdom.[10] Be well, and pray for me, Most Reverent One.

---

[7] What additional work the editor needed to do to ready the *Life* for publication is unclear, and so perhaps *syntáxas*—as I have translated, "put it together"— here has the sense of "make a copy."

[8] Hypatius was the first abbot, and Callinicus, the disciple of Hypatius, was perhaps second abbot. Callinicus composed the *Life* and bequeathed it to the unnamed third abbot, from whom the writer of the dedication had received it.

[9] Aspiration is adding a rough breathing (an "h") to the beginning of a word that begins with a vowel.

[10] See 1 Cor 1:20.

Prologue

1. It is because of the yearning of Your Reverence, a Christ-loving priest,[1] a yearning that God implanted in you who deserve it—for your actions have convinced us that Christ has made you a new Cornelius[2]— 2. and it is because of your trust, most reverent and genuine brothers in Christ,[3] that in loving Christ and being borne along by a spiritual yearning and being impelled Godward while simultaneously pestering me, a slave of Christ,[4] over and over again, your entreaties would appeal to my mercy—or rather, your yearning would urge me to enjoy the spiritual altar and fulfill the greatest service— 3. that I depict for Your Reverence, as best I can, the regimen of our father among the saints, Hypatius, doing so for the glory of God and the honor of the saints who fought the good fight[5] and proved pleasing to God. 4. Indeed, with Christ's grace working alongside [me], through your prayers, I trust in my God that Christ will let me publicize Saint Hypatius's singular and august life. 5. Whatever wonders of God came about through him I have personally beheld; whatever I heard from those who were disciples before me; whatever he personally narrated while glorifying God and giving thanks to him—the kind of gifts that God

---

[1] According to what the editor said above (Ded.5), this section shows Callinicus addressing the third abbot of the Rufinianae.

[2] See Acts 10:1-48.

[3] Callinicus now addresses the monks of the Rufinianae as a collective.

[4] "Slave of Christ" or, more frequently, "slave of God" is a synonym for "monk" throughout this text. For further discussion, see the introduction to this volume.

[5] 1 Tim 6:12; 2 Tim 4:7.

reserves for those who love him according to what has been written, "I will tell of all your wonders"[6]— 6. these are what I am eager to publicize to Your Love of God with my treatise. Consequently, let us and all who are lovers of Christ, all who have been made better, glorify God and honor the saints. Zealous in virtue,[7] let us be eager to imitate them 7. so that we are found to be co-heirs[8] in eternal life, when the righteous shall shine like the sun[9] according to what has been written, "Imitate their faith as you contemplate the outcome of their life."[10]

8. When need be, he was even compelled to offer guidance to his own disciples for their own good; he would always say to them, "Children, if I were a smith or a carpenter, wouldn't you imitate me to learn the craft? 9. So too now, become like me; learn fear of the Lord and how God is pleased."

10. [He said] the same thing to monks coming from afar as he did to visiting friends and admirers. There are a great number of people in the world who are fervent in spirit[11] and who thirstily seek how to find a faithful man who also possesses the gift of turning souls toward the fear of God, according to [the scriptural verse] that says, 11. "Let those who fear you and who know your testimony turn to me."[12] "For it is a hard task to find a faithful man."[13] 12. When these people came into his monastery and compelled him to teach, he took it to heart that God summoned him to the task of bettering and saving souls; when hard-pressed, he used to say, 13. "If you are seeking something from me, you will find it in the God-inspired Scripture. 14. But as for me, corresponding to my deficiency, whatever the Lord supplies for the restoration of

---

[6] Ps 74:3(75:1).

[7] Gal 4:18.

[8] See Rom 8:7.

[9] Matt 13:43.

[10] Heb 13:7.

[11] Rom 12:11.

[12] Ps 118(119):79.

[13] Prov 20:6.

your souls[14] and my own benefit is what I, a wretch, will teach you in both words and deeds as God has granted to me—or rather, the Lord will teach you through my humility. For what do we have that we did not receive from God?"[15]

15. Just as he would earnestly offer us guidance while crying, he would claim that it was for his own benefit; he was overjoyed at the distribution of the divine word. 16. When he began to speak, grace so inspired him that the hearer of his speech was immediately stung and regarded it as guidance from not a human being but the Lord. 17. Indeed, the Lord spoke through him too; indeed, God spoke in his saint according to what has been written, "That I may give grace to those who hear."[16] 18. Later I will tell you about his teaching, but the occasion summons us to start again and to render the story of his most noble life and valiant regimen from the beginning.

[14] Eph 4:12.
[15] 1 Cor 4:7.
[16] Eph 4:29.

Chapter 1

1. He was born in Phrygia. His homeland was, by its nature, an educational center for literary training. His parents were well-born and God-fearers; being a scholasticus,[1] his father gave him sufficient literary training. 2. They schooled him in a traditional curriculum as well as in the Lord's admonition[2]—to behave with fear and to remain subordinate to his parents. From childhood, his holiness had been a natural characteristic, well-raised as he was in the fear of God. 3. He possessed compunction and yearning; he was always on the lookout for an opportunity to leave and escape either to the church or to the monastery in order to find reverent men. 4. For there were none yet around in Phrygia back then except for maybe one or two, and if a church could be found anywhere, the clergy were sluggish, as was generally the case in rural areas. 5. That's why, even up till now, almost everyone who had been thoroughly educated about him—having heard the stories about him and having been amazed that a man like him came from their own region—became Christian, while some even emulated him in virtue.[3]

6. However, back then, there was no monastery in the shining city of Constantine except for that of the great Isaac, whom Saint Dalmatios succeeded.[4] 7. Well, one day, after his father had bludgeoned him, [Hypatius] resolved to move away from his parents;

---

[1] Technically, the term designates a lawyer, but it may be the case that Callinicus simply uses the term generally for a cultured, learned person.

[2] See Luke 2:51.

[3] See Gal 4:18.

[4] On Isaac and Dalmatios, see the introduction to this volume.

he made a two- or three-day journey, as he told it, and came upon a church and heard the holy Gospel saying that the Lord said, 8. "Whoever leaves father, mother, brothers, sisters, wife, children, and property for my sake will receive a hundredfold and inherit eternal life"[5] (for in addition to his parents, he left his little sister too). 9. And so, as if inspired by God at hearing this in the Gospel, and especially when his aim had gained further clarity, he found some travelers and traveled with them to Thrace.

[5] Matt 19:29.

Chapter 2

1. When they arrived in Thrace without coming across any lodging, they spent the night on a mountain where they were taken by surprise: the mountain was covered on one side with foliage from the trees, and the place was frightening because of the demons who spent their nights there. 2. Those [demons] who came to cast insults at [Hypatius and the travelers] would say to themselves, "We can do nothing to them, for there is a child with them who has received authority over us." [The travelers] heard this in their sleep and became unsettled; when they woke up, they heard among the trees noise from the demons fleeing. 3. The child of God also knew what had happened, for he was eighteen years old.[1] 4. At daybreak, they asked him if he knew what had happened. When he said no,[2] they gave thanks to the Lord and wondered what kind of Christian child God had given them as a traveling companion. 5. Noticing how he always kept his eyes looking downward and how he comported himself with reverence, they entrusted him to a certain housemaster; indeed, [Hypatius] was ashamed to go anywhere by himself. 6. Upon receiving him, [the housemaster] gave him sheep to tend. This ought not strike us strange, for God had proclaimed this about him in advance, that he was destined to shepherd Christ's spiritual sheep too. 7. We are not ignorant, though, that the holy Moses, Jacob, and David also tended to sheep.

---

[1] The possible significance of his age is twofold. It could indicate that he had fully come into adulthood, or it could bear a symbolic numerological meaning, as the number eighteen is written in Greek as IHʹ, the first two letters of Jesus' name in Greek, thus linking Hypatius's identity with Christ's.

[2] In a statement of humility.

Well, since he was tending sheep, he also lifted his voice in song, as happened among shepherds.

8. There was a church nearby, and when its priest heard his voice, he urged him to leave the housemaster. He promised to teach [Hypatius] psalms, to let him sing psalms in church, and to give him to those living the monastic life, if that's what he wanted. 9. Since this is what he yearned for, he gave himself over. As he began to sing psalms in church, then, [the priest] marveled at [Hypatius's] proficiency and how he diligently learned the psalms.

10. [Hypatius] was unwilling to partake in wine. With nearly all the clergy drinking wine with their daytime meals, he saw how one would pass out and another behave sloppily, as tends to happen in the country, and he watched the laypeople not get any assistance. He was thoroughly disgusted.

Chapter 3

1. In the mist of his worry, [Hypatius] begged God to think him worthy of dwelling among the reverent; in response to his prayer God dispatched to Constantinople a certain soldier by the name of Jonah, an Armenian by race, who had been spurred by God to renounce the world.[1] 2. From that point onward Jonah frequently begged the tribune of his military unit to be discharged, but he was not, and one day, he carried a small bundle of wood on his shoulders and a flame in his hand; when the most pious emperor Arcadius[2] was making a public procession, [Jonah] approached him and said, 3. "Until now I have served Your Sovereignty, but from now on I want to serve Christ. Order my discharge. 4. If you won't, you have the authority to burn your slave on this.[3] For I cannot do anything else."

5. As the emperor saw his pious intent right away, he ordered [Jonah] discharged. And [Jonah] immediately left the city, and, after he left, he pitched a tent for himself on the mountainside—not at all far from the church where the slave of God[4] was! 6. While residing in a tent, [Jonah] lived off plants. Realizing what he was doing, the rural folks around there helped him build his cell and cultivated the small plot of land for him. 7. Because he sang psalms and prayed and fasted and trained in every virtue belonging to

---

[1] "Renouncing the world" or "making a renunciation" in this text and other monastic writings is a synonym for taking up the ascetic life. On Jonah, see the introduction to this volume.

[2] Eastern emperor of the Roman Empire (377–408). He was the son of Theodosius I (347–395) and the father of Theodosius II (401–450).

[3] That is, the wood he was carrying.

[4] That is, Hypatius.

one living the monastic life—for he was acquainted with [monastic virtue], having learned it from his own homeland; indeed, the Armenians fervently worshiped God—one after another began to join up with him in order to be enslaved to God.

8. When that friend of God, Hypatius, heard about [Jonah], he immediately took leave of the priest and other [clergy members] and went out to [Jonah], saying, "I want to be enslaved to God too." And right away, [Jonah] accepted him. 9. Those who discharged [Hypatius] were really quite distressed on account of his reverence and because he had stayed in the church longer than everyone. He had been there for twenty years when he approached Jonah, the slave of God. 10. And so, as others were joining up with them too, they began to prepare both a garden for planting seed and a plot of land for constructing a monastery so that it could house [up to] eighty brothers and become a great fortress. 11. Because the Huns were close by and could easily plunder, people in those regions used to build fortresses. 12. The sacred teacher Jonah gave all of them instruction, but Hypatius was so engrossed in his discipline that he surpassed everyone—and nearly their superior!—when it came to fasting, vigilance, psalmody, prayer, obedience, tranquility, humility, poverty, and every virtue. As a result, everyone benefited from him and glorified God, and his superior adored him and rejoiced at his regimen.

Chapter 4

1. So much did he train in tranquility by fasting and praying that everyone desired to hear a word from him and begged him to instruct them for their benefit. 2. This he rejected, saying, "In the world, I was a slave, but now I come to be deemed worthy of being your slave." At that, he fell at his superior's feet and said, "Order me to minister exclusively to the afflicted." 3. For he used to claim that he did this because he had heard in the holy Gospel, "I have chosen this commandment of the Lord, who spoke to those on his right side, 4. 'Come, you who are blessed by my father, take as your inheritance the kingdom prepared for you.'[1] For I was hungry, and you gave me something to eat. I was thirsty, and you gave me something to drink. I was a stranger, and you gathered with me. I was naked, and you clothed me. I was weak, and you looked over me. I was in prison, and you came to me.'[2] And when they said, 'Lord, when did we know you like that, and when did we do these things?'[3] he answered, 'Truly, truly, I say to you, whatever you did for one of the least of my brothers, you did to me.' "[4]

5. After receiving the order from his superior, [Hypatius] demonstrated such enthusiasm that he went out a far distance under the pretense of examining the regions' potential for sowing. 6. Upon finding some rural folk who were poor, in sickly condition, cast out on the road, as he told us—for he used to tell us stories involving Saint Jonah—he took and carried them on his shoulders and laid

[1] Callinicus omits the Gospel's phrase "from the foundation of the world."
[2] Matt 25:34-36.
[3] See Matt 25:37-39.
[4] Matt 25:40.

them at the [monastery's] gate. As he was entering, he said to the Abba, "Some people brought a sick person to the gate, and, leaving him there, they went away!" 7. After being ordered to do so, he brought him in. [Hypatius] gave the person, whether injured or ill, a bath and cared for him as needed; laying out a bed, he gave him rest and fed him the suitable foods. If the ill person needed to be anointed, [Hypatius] would announce it to the Abba—for he was a priest—and get him to perform the anointing with blessed oil. Within a few days, he would discharge a healthy person, with God working with him just as it has been written, "God works with everyone who enacts the good."[5] 8. We heard this too from the brothers there: if anyone had recently come down with a fever, Hypatius would go out to examine and investigate him and with his hand secretly make the precious cross and with his mind pray strenuously, saying to the brother, "Get up, there is nothing wrong with you, go back to your job." 9. These words he would say with such faithfulness that, immediately relieved, the sick person felt better. Whenever someone stood up after eagerly listening to him, he would remain healthy and not have anything wrong, with God supplying [the cure].

[5] Rom 2:10, 8:28.

Chapter 5

1. And so, while doing these things for the brothers and everyone else, he slept on a rush mat and practiced self-control to such a degree that he even frequently took up the five-day [fast]. 2. Quite often, he was pestered by the demon of youth, ghastly pleasure, that troubles young men and tries to subvert them unless they exercise caution. 3. And if he continued to struggle with self-control after he made his renunciation, he would continuously implore God to come do battle against those who battled [Hypatius], [to help him] endure in faithfulness and succeed in these practices of self-control, endurance, love, and humility, so that the battle would not cause him despair and that he might remain faithful: "If I'm not set free today, I will be set free tomorrow; if not within five years, then within ten."[1] He simply would not surrender and flee the arena; rather, he stood firm and endured. 4. For "he who endures to the end will be saved."[2] As the battle approached, he simply would cross himself and immediately turn to pray. While watching his struggle, God sent his grace and liberated his soul. 5. Even if our own quest for God is particularly sluggish, let us not lose faith and give up but endure. God knows what is good for us, according to [the scriptural verse] that says, "If you keep faith that you will see the good things of the Lord, then wait for the Lord."[3] 6. If anyone were to refuse this and not renounce living his life, let

---

[1] This quotation, although attributed to Hypatius, originates in Pseudo-Macarius, *Spiritual Homily* 26.11. On the correspondence between the Pseudo-Macariana and the *Life of Hypatius*, see the introduction to this volume.

[2] See Matt 10:22.

[3] See Ps 26(27):14. Here "wait" is the same verb as "endure" in the previous sentence (*hypoménōmen* and *hypómeinon*).

him go about the custom of getting married whenever he finally reaches maturity, living solemnly with the fear of the Lord. For [marriage] is a fine thing from God. 7. Thus, let us fortify ourselves lest Satan tempt us: "for each has his own spiritual gift from God, one in one way, another in another way."[4]

8. Well, there was one day when Hypatius had been especially engaged in this battle while not drinking anything for fifty days in the middle of [summertime] heat; he became constipated, and his lips began to crack with dryness. 9. When the brothers saw him, they informed the archimandrite [Jonah], who had been silent from his nightly prayers. He mixed a cup of wine with a morsel [of bread] and, before everyone, called out to him, "Hypatius!" He answered, "Bless me." He said, "Come over here, accept this blessing and drink it!" [Hypatius] never partook of wine. 10. Comporting himself with a fatherly disposition and knowing that obedience would engender life,[5] with faithfulness he accepted it and drank, thereby making himself more able to tolerate the battle.

<hr>

[4] 1 Cor 7:7.
[5] See John 12:52.

Chapter 6

1. [Hypatius] used to tell [the disciples] this story. "The barbarians, who used to attack Thrace quite often, surrounded our stronghold, and God, who always defends his slaves as they pray, chased them away. 2. Indeed, [the slaves of God] had a small opening through which they tossed stones to injure just one but that caused the others, waving their whips as a signal [to each other], to get back on their horses and retreat. 3. When the action died down, the peasants who had been plundered and had nothing left ran to the monastery in search of anything that could help them. 4. Lord Jonah then traveled to the great city[1] and spoke to the nobility with frankness: 'In Thrace, the poor who were plundered are hungry, and they are bothering me. Send them provisions.'

5. "As if to a father, Rufinus[2] and the other important men listened to him; with God's help, everyone set their mind to loading the ships with grain and seed and then sending them to [Jonah] so that he could dole it out to them. 6. For as soon as he entered the city, all the wealthy people asked that he give them a blessing by praying in their house. 7. So zealous a man was he that he rebuked all the noble people to their faces. If he discovered that they had committed a crime, he advocated for the injured party even if it meant [his own] death and simultaneously admonished [the nobility] by saying, 'The tears of the injured are an indictment against criminals.'[3] 8. But those whom he benefited honored him

---

[1] Constantinople.

[2] This is probably the Rufinus who built the complex of buildings that would become the Rufinianae. For more on this political figure, see the introduction to this volume.

[3] See Sir 35:18.

as a true slave of God while simultaneously standing awestruck that he received such grace from the Lord despite being unlettered and uncultivated."[4]

---

[4] See Acts 4:13.

Chapter 7

1. Hypatius's father heard about these things and, since a judgment was coming against him in a legal matter, went from his own country to the city and immediately ran up to Thrace and sought out the fortress, the name for which was Halmyrissos.[1] Once he found it, he looked for his son. 2. For he was an old and a very distinguished man. When the monks got wind of this, they said, "Didn't Hypatius once say that he was a slave?" And they all rejoiced with the Abba because he had done this[2] with God's help and with humility. 3. When [Hypatius] heard that his father had come, he did not want to be noticed by him. After a while, though, he felt compelled; so he conversed with him and embraced him and then joined him in prayer. It was from him that [Hypatius] learned of his mother's passing. 4. He realized that his father needed assistance in his legal matter and that, during the subsequent time [when he would be gone], the brothers could take care of the liturgy and farm work since their Abba had grown old and, because of his old age, would linger in the city [for a bit longer].[3] And so he sent word to the archimandrite and accompanied his father to the city and stayed with him at the suburban residence of a certain Eleutherus.[4] With God's help, he assisted [his father] in his legal matter and then gave him instruction before sending him back to his region. After his return, [his father] came to his end in peace.

---

[1] Possibly Salmydesseus (near modern Kıyıköy), on the Black Sea, approximately sixty miles northwest of the Bosporus.

[2] That is, denied his illustrious background.

[3] That is, Hypatius's father showed up while Jonah was in Constantinople arranging the grain shipments (see 6.5).

[4] This person is unknown.

Chapter 8

1. Hypatius was joined by a certain ascetic, well known in his own right, by the name of Timothy. He too was so reverent and devoted to virtue that he therefore fastened himself to Hypatius because he was a slave of God. 2. To them was also added another monk by the name of Moschius, and they became a trio of brothers, slaves of God. 3. And so, when they were staying at the suburban residence, Hypatius said to them, "I am accustomed to dwelling on a mountain, not in a city." And they answered, "We go where you go." 4. After he passed through Chalcedon, he kept going westward, looking for a mountain or a cave. He went three miles and found a church dedicated to an apostle with a monastery next to it, both of which the blessed Rufinus had built after receiving from Rome the remains of the holy apostles Peter and Paul, which he magnificently deposited once he built the martyrium. Rufinus's urn also lay nearby. 5. Having founded the monastery, Rufinus made it a dwelling-place for Egyptian monks, but when he died, the Egyptians left it and went back to their native country.[1] 6. From then on, the monastery remained deserted so that it no longer looked like a monastery; in fact, a demon even entered and took up residence there. 7. Many people tried to live there, but because of the demon and because of the winter mud, they had no opportunity to furnish it and did not have the fortitude to stay. Yes, the place was quite remote.

8. When Hypatius came and learned that a terrible demon dwelled within, he boiled up with the faith of Christ, sealed himself [with the sign of the cross], and uttered a prayer. He went and

---

[1] On the buildings of the Rufinianae, see the introduction to this volume.

made himself a neighbor to the topmost and holy apostles, by whose intercessions we have been shown mercy. 9. When his two brothers heard about this, they went to him; they shared the same disposition as he did and possessed serious discipline. 10. For both Hypatius and Timothy challenged [each other to see] who could fast better, or pray harder, or humble himself more, or show greater mercy to the poor. 11. Indeed, they supported [each other] with their own hands: one worked with [animal] hair and the other at baskets, while the third [tended to the] garden. There was both a courtyard surrounded by cells and a chapel that had gone long neglected. Amongst [these cells], they found a small cell where they could stay and work at maintaining tranquility. 12. But whenever they wanted to pray or sing psalms in the chapel, they caught sight of something like a fiery ball circling the entire building, thunderously attacking them, and still, they were steadfast and persisted in prayer. 13. The structure was large and deserted, causing it to fill with snow during the winter. With only one day left to survive, two [of them] went out into the city to sell their hand-made products and thereby secure sustenance. 14. But a certain woman—wealthy and entirely Christian, who had prayed among the apostles[2]—overheard as she was passing by that there was a monk in the monastery; she entered by herself, leaving her children outside; she put the ascetic to the test, for she was an expertly trained[3] deacon, and falling before him, she said, "Christian! Bless me and receive me so that I might stay with you." 15. But [Hypatius] grew angry and screamed out, "Get back from me, Satan![4] Did you come here to make me run away? We don't have many days left. Keep whatever is here and stay however long you want." 16. He ran away as fast as he could.[5] Then she motioned toward her children and

---

[2] That is, in the Church of the Holy Apostles in the Rufinianae.

[3] Or "expertly ascetic."

[4] Matt 16:23.

[5] The presentation Callinicus makes about Hypatius's anxiety and hostility toward the woman reflects widespread stereotypes in early Christian monastic texts of women as worldly, untrustworthy temptresses.

grabbed hold of him, saying, "I tested you to know whether you were truly a monk. Go into your cell and pray for me." 17. Since she knew that [the monks] were three in number, she immediately sent them goods sufficient for survival.

Chapter 9

1. With them being genuine slaves to the Lord in love, the Hater of Good could not contain himself and set many schemes in motion against them; he proved unable to chase them out with either fear or any other machination—for they endured and remained there, and those who renounced the world were added to their ranks—and finally he contrived a scheme to provoke Hypatius and Timothy against each other. 2. Hypatius, being wise, even yielded to him—after all, the place was his—but [Timothy], being less incorruptible and spiritual, did not want to act as ruler and manager [to the monks], but neither would he let Hypatius do so. 3. As time passed, Hypatius felt overwhelmed and yielded to him; he gave up the place to [Timothy]. After running into a brother from his first monastery, he returned with him to Thrace. 4. A paralytic man who had been disabled by a demon lay outside as they exited, and he asked them for alms. When Hypatius saw him, he was moved and asked, "What happened to you?" 5. And upon learning that he had been disabled by a demon, [Hypatius] said to the one who was with him, "Let's go get him, and let's both bring him to the church." 6. He took the lamp's oil, uttered a prayer, and then anointed him. Immediately the Lord gave him strength, and once [the paralytic] recovered his health, he followed them. 7. Consequently, the locals who saw what had happened chased behind them and, touching the edges of their cloaks,[1] begged [Hypatius and his companions] to watch over them too. 8. However, they responded, "We are only sinful human beings,[2] but it was the Lord who healed this man."

[1] Matt 9:20, with parallels in Mark 6:56 and Luke 8:44.
[2] See Acts 14:15.

9. And so they made their journey and went to the [Thracian] monastery. Once the brothers and the archimandrite [Jonah] heard what happened and saw the person who had been healed, they glorified God and said, "Before he left here, we knew that God had given him the gift of healings." 10. The man who had been healed, however, made his renunciation and, after becoming a slave to the Lord, died. Hypatius, in the meantime, exhorted the venerable Lord Jonah to give him a cell for maintaining tranquility.

Chapter 10

1. Timothy along with the other brothers, however, went looking for Hypatius, nearly in tears. Knowing that Jonah, the slave of God, had gone into the city, they lingered, imploring him to make Lord Hypatius come back to them from Thrace. 2. Meanwhile, Abba Jonah, who was indisposed and having a hard time of it, saw someone say to him during the night, "If Hypatius does not come, you will not regain your health." 3. And instantly he revealed [Hypatius's location] to the brothers so that they might send for him. Having learned what had been revealed to the Abba and that he was being looked for, those who had assembled exhorted him to leave. But when he was unwilling to do so, they forced him and sent him with another brother. 4. And so they went on their way, and, at a certain spot, they performed the third-hour prayer. While praying, then, out of thin air, they heard a voice saying, "Hypatius, go to the Rufinianae, for I have made you a light for the Gentiles to the end of the earth."[1] 5. Well, they were terrified, and they prostrated themselves, petitioning God for a long time. They finally got up, and Hypatius started to grumble, as if he was going to refuse, but the one who was trembling alongside him said to him, "Come on, man! What are you talking about? You are going to get us devoured [by the Devil]!"[2]

6. So when they came to Lord Jonah [in Constantinople] and saw him having a hard time of it, virtually unable to speak, Hypatius touched him, performed a prayer, and gave him food; immediately he felt greater relief. For he had not eaten anything for days. 7. As

---

[1] Isa 49:6; Acts 13.
[2] See 1 Pet 5:8.

he gained his strength back day by day, he exhorted Abba Hypatius to go to the brothers at the Rufinianae and summoned Timothy. He gave them advice, saying, "Don't be surprised.[3] There was also a dispute among the holy apostles."[4] 8. They embraced each other and made peace. [The brothers at the Rufinianae] finally accepted that they would have Hypatius as a father, and he governed them according to the directive of the Lord, who, out of thin air, spoke to him. He was then forty years old.

[3] 1 Pet 4:12.
[4] See Acts 15:39.

Chapter 11

1. The monasteries of the blessed Isaac,[1] who was alive back then and leading them to zeal, formed into a federation; from this effort, neighboring monasteries came to exist in the city itself, in the suburban areas, and in further exurban areas. Living within them were more than one hundred and fifty brothers, glorifying God. 2. The blessed Isaac continued to oversee them as if they were his own children. For these reasons, during his frequent visits to Hypatius, he used to give instructions, saying, 3. "Glory to God, who allows slaves of God to dwell among the products of Rufinus's labor! Hear me now, child, I acknowledge you so that God may glorify you. Whether you have little or much, don't let a stranger pass by who has become aggrieved against you, but open your door to every stranger." 4. After praying together and giving [Hypatius] a blessing, [Isaac] left, and wherever he knew there to be people lacking in the basic necessities for life, if he did not have them himself, he would speak to the elites and the Christians, and they would send them. For [Isaac] was honored by all, and they listened to him like a father.

5. Likewise, even the great John,[2] who was bishop back then, paid [Hypatius] such tremendous deference and cherished the

---

[1] Isaac is also mentioned at 1.6. For more, see the introduction to this volume.

[2] John Chrysostom (ca. 349–407) was a monk, then priest at Antioch, then bishop of Constantinople. His career was interrupted when Bishop Theophilus of Alexandria orchestrated an investigation into his orthodoxy at the "Synod of the Oak," a location very close to the Rufinianae. He refused to attend and was found guilty in absentia, for which he was sent into exile in Cucusus and then Pithyus. He died during his exile. In 438, Emperor Theodosius II and others rehabilitated his standing within the orthodox tradition. His remains were

slaves of God! In his deeds, he truly was a bishop, the light of the church, the precious jewel in the crown of the faith, someone who did nothing unworthy of God, someone who deservedly received the throne and the grace from God, someone whose way of life distinguished him. 6. For having been exiled to some place far from well-known quarters, he died after praying. 7. Once a few years had passed, the most pious emperor Theodosius recalled his remains with great glory, as if they belonged to great and holy martyrs.

8. But considering things suitable to life, [John] cried out to the reverent ones and said, "You owe an explanation for why you are concealing yourselves. By refusing appointments [to ecclesiastical office] and by causing others whom we do not know to be appointed [instead], you were not putting your lamp on the lamp-stand!"[3] 9. For one of the monks who had been appointed but who had been unwilling to have a bishop's hand placed on him bit the bishop's finger.

---

brought back and housed in the Church of the Apostles at Constantinople. For more, see the introduction to this volume.

[3] See Matt 5:15 with parallels in Mark 4:21 and Luke 8:16.

Chapter 12

1. Hypatius, then, went to the Rufinianae with Timothy, and they attained such an intensity in discipline and love for one another that many, upon laying eyes upon them, emulated them and renounced life. In a short time, they gradually gathered together, and there were thirty monks with them. 2. While they were persevering in their psalmody, prayer, and hospitality, the Lord also drove out the demon from the monastery and bestowed the gift of healings to Hypatius. 3. And so because Hypatius had compassion for all, he was loved by all, for he suffered with those who suffered, and he laid hold of the afflicted, saying, "It is written, 'To those in prison, be as if you were imprisoned with them, and to the mistreated, as if you too were mistreated in the body,'[1] 'crying with those who cry and rejoicing with those who rejoice.'"[2] 4. Among them was a certain cubicularius by the name of Urbicius;[3] he was completely Christian, and, when he learned about Saint Hypatius, he became quite a close friend to him. He discovered that a certain person was being terrorized by a brother who was wealthy—indeed, the one drove the other brother mad and, after locking him up in some place, tried to murder him. Well, when the noble Urbicius learned

[1] See Heb 13:3.

[2] Rom 12:15.

[3] Urbicius was an imperial official who had several posts over the course of an extremely long career (as cubicularius, he served as a chamberlain in the imperial palace). As several episodes in the text indicate, he was a major financial supporter of Hypatius and the Rufinianae. He died at the beginning of the sixth century. See J. R. Martindale, *The Prosopography of the Later Roman Empire, Volume II: A.D. 395–527* (Cambridge: Cambridge University Press, 1980), 1188–90, Urbicius 1.

of this, he grabbed hold of him and then brought him to and set him before Saint Hypatius.

5. But when some of his slaves mulled it over, they said to the cubicularius, "If he dies in the monastery, the monastery can lay claim to his property."[4] 6. Convinced by these words, then, he went to the monastery and, rushing like a lion, he went inside, looking to take the man and send him back to his own home. 7. But the man (Aetius was his name)[5] was in state of shock, and his body was terribly weak. And so Hypatius prayed for him to recover his health, fed him, and tended to his needs since he could not use his own hands to take nourishment.

8. When Urbicius went looking to take him and send him back to his home, Hypatius said to him, "God made me the man's body-guard, and I cannot give him to you lest he later die on the road, since he is so sick. 9. Let him recover his health with God providing it, and then, afterwards, take him. But if you are afraid on account of his wealth, I will put it in writing that I will not take anything from it. However, I am not handing him over to you. If you've got the guts to come in and grab him, do it." 10. Standing at a loss, [Urbicius] went away upset, but Hypatius took care of the man, and, by praying, anointing him with blessed oil, and offering relief, he made him come to his senses, with God furnishing health to him. 11. While he spent his time in the monastery, he glorified God and thanked Hypatius; afterwards, once a long stretch of time had passed, he came to his end.

12. Immediately [after Aetius's death], Hypatius informed the cubicularius, and, after asking, the cubicularius received the man's wealth. Thereupon, Urbicius gave thanks and came to embrace the slave of God as a father; he made an offering but was denied.

---

[4] The slaves are referring here to *Theodosian Code* 5.3.1 (December 15, 434), which notes that the property of any intestate clergy member or monk, without children or spouse, shall go to the church or monastic community to which he belonged.

[5] This person is otherwise unknown.

13. Finally, [Hypatius] nevertheless consented to his renovating the monastery; employing craftsmen from his fellow laborers and brothers,[6] he repaired the house of God and built both the chapel and additional cells, so that [the monastery] became the glory of God, and more brothers could dwell in it.

[6] That is, other monks.

Chapter 13

1. The Christ-loving Hypatius made an extremely austere cell for himself, in which he confined himself for the forty days [of Lent], with the door sealed by mud. It was through a small opening in the door that he took bread every second day; through it, he also conversed with passersby and benefited them. 2. When he emerged on Holy Easter, his facial expression made him look like an angel of God, filled with divine grace, and immediately he went to the [church of] the Holy Apostles.[1] He was ordained a priest at the holy apostolic church after the blessed Bishop Philotheos[2] forcibly ordained him. 3. While he was ministering the divine offering[3] he loudly groaned and cried out to God so that those who heard were deeply affected by his tears. 4. Each Sunday that he led the service for the holy apostles, fear and knowledge developed in everyone, and with deed and word he corrected everyone. Even the clergy members revered him as a father.

[1] See 8.4.
[2] This person is otherwise unknown.
[3] The Eucharist.

Chapter 14

1. Frequently, during [Hypatius's] confinement, many secrets were revealed to him, which he did not wish to talk about. Yet we came to know about them in this way: if there was any brother who felt despondent because he was afflicted by thoughts or some other affliction, [Hypatius] would render benefit to his soul by summoning him and giving him guidance. 2. In those situations, [Hypatius might have] said about a certain newly arrived brother, "So-and-so steals [food] and eats without a blessing." 3. A brother would then begin to watch over him and find him doing this. And being corrected with a holy guidance, he was corrected but claiming that he had done so in ignorance. 4. For [Hypatius] had seen that a serpent coiled all around him from his feet up to his neck and that the serpent was peeking into the brother's mouth. 5. Frequently, during the Holy Easter, when [the brother] left his cell, he could be found hoarding the food given to him in his cell, for he would partake of a little bit and then save the rest.[1]

---

[1] That is, he was not participating in the Lenten fast.

Chapter 15

1. At another time again, the domesticus[1] of the man Urbicius,[2] someone by the name of Alcimus,[3] who had practiced magic, became half-desiccated. He went with Urbicius and begged Hypatius that he might get a healing. 2. When the slave of God prayed and anointed him with oil, the Lord healed him within a few days.

3. And in the meantime, he beheld in his cell the Hater of Good in a luminous cloak, speaking to him: "Hypatius, why have you taken this person from me? For he was handed over to me a long time ago." 4. But Hypatius responded to him, "The Lord will punish you, Devil, and render your evil machinations impotent. For how long will you wage war against the human race, finding nourishment in the scents of sacrifices and filth ever since you were cast from such glory? For how long will you not repent of your evil deeds?" 5. He answered, "Were I to repent, my dear Hypatius, would God welcome me [back] into my former position?" 6. Hypatius said to the Devil, "That wouldn't be right in your case, Devil. Wouldn't you be satisfied that the saints are begging God to welcome you as just another repentant sinner?" 7. He responded, "I have such great authority in the world, and you say to me that I would be just another sinner? You utter nice words, Hypatius." 8. Upon saying this, and after the saint prayed, he vanished. So the cubicularis with the domesticus glorified God and, giving thanks, embraced the slave of God. 9. Then on behalf of his own soul, the cubicularis, who would [later] become a prefect, erected a

---

[1] This could be a palace official or perhaps merely a household slave.
[2] See 12.4.
[3] This person is otherwise unknown.

mausoleum, with the most pious emperor also vowing contributions [to the project], into which the remains of deceased brothers would be deposited. Then, once he was succeeded [by someone else], [the cubicularis] could again devote himself [to spiritual pursuits].

Chapter 16

1. The blessed Jonah came to visit Hypatius too, and, after praying with him, he blessed him, saying, "I came to see you, my legitimate child. For I am about to travel the road of the fathers. 2. I hold you as [my] right hand after God, since after you left me, you made a monastery for yourself." And once he spoke these words, he returned to the monastery and came to rest in peace. 3. Hypatius told the story that when he was in Thrace, a brother struck him, and his mouth began to bleed; when the ninth hour came,[1] the one who struck him was stung by his conscience, and he did not receive a blessing. 4. While eating, the Abba noticed the absence of that brother and, having learned about the deed, summoned him and said to Hypatius, "Make peace." 5. And Hypatius answered, "A little while ago, he filled my mouth with blood, and now I am supposed to come and show him affection?" 6. He said these words to teach us that, even if someone happened to get mad at his brother, he ought to change course immediately, just as the Lord also taught us in the Gospel.[2]

---

[1] Three o'clock in the afternoon, when the monks would take their meal, as becomes clear in the next sentence.

[2] Matt 5:24.

Chapter 17

1. And when he came to practice monasticism in this place,[1] he said, "I found a clay vessel, made it warm, and dipped my bread [in it]. That's how impoverished I was. 2. And another time, when a stranger came and we had just one loaf of bread, I went elsewhere for a meeting so that the loaf of bread would suffice for the two brothers with me and the stranger. 3. And when I returned there, I found that they had eaten, and they asked me, saying, 'Abba Hypatius, did you eat?' And I answered them, 'Yes.' 4. And again, the brothers said to me as I came to the monastery, 'Lord, have you eaten?' And I answered them, 'Yes.' 5. And when I learned that God had sent other loaves of bread, then I made my confession to them and ate.

6. "On one of the days when we had no bread left, while I was sitting on the front porch at noon, I was deeply upset, and I fell asleep. Then, I saw a noble old man come; he kicked me in my side and said to me, 'Hypatius, are you upset because you don't have any loaves of bread? Get up and don't be upset! Indeed, from now on, your table won't be missing any loaves of bread—neither for you nor for those with you.'" 8. And he convinced us by saying, "Really, my children, from that moment, I decided to give, as often as I could, whatever I had to the poor so that I could see if anything remained, and never did anything remain on account of the one who supplied it. Consequently, the Scripture was fulfilled that said, 'Those who seek the Lord will lack no good.'"[2]

[1] That is, the Rufinianae.
[2] Ps 33:11 (34:10).

Chapter 18

1. While they were working, they made a loaf of bread by their own exertions and provided it to others too. And if anyone made an offering, then [Hypatius] would eagerly distribute it to the poor, so that the Scripture was fulfilled that said, "Their hands have supplied enough for both me and those with me."[1] 2. Within a few years, fifty brothers had gathered and lived with him; after Hypatius successively instructed them and many others, he made them his disciples. They came to despise the world, and then they became monks.

3. Among this initial group was a certain [man] by the name of Aquilas,[2] who, along with his five children and his wife,[3] made his renunciation. He put the wife in a cell to practice monasticism far away from himself. 4. One of his children, called Benjamin, devoted himself entirely to the Lord. Indeed, when Abba Hypatius was indisposed [with illness] and was declining in health, the child Benjamin stood with pain in his soul; he groaned aloud and said, 5. "Lord, because of the brothers and the needy, take me instead of Abba!" 6. And so, in three days, the child grew weak and came to rest in the Lord. Likewise, Aquilas, who had conducted himself nobly, came to his end at a good old age.

[1] See Acts 20:34.
[2] This person is otherwise unknown.
[3] Literally, "freed woman." The term indicates that she was formerly enslaved.

Chapter 19

1. Water flowed in the aqueduct near the monastery, and the brothers used it. Some people, though, threw their filthy waste into the water—whether out of ignorance or by the design of a demon, only they know. 2. However, the brothers got sick because of it and were terribly afflicted because those who were responsible kept doing it. 3. Like a father for his own children, the saint got upset, fasted, prayed, and exhorted the Master Christ to give them water or to stop the treacherous men. 4. And after the third day [of fasting and praying], he saw three men in luminous clothing speaking to one another: "Which spot should we show to the Abba, that he might dig a ditch and find water for the brothers?" 5. Accordingly, one of them took Hypatius by the hand, brought him to the place, and said to him, "As soon as you begin to dig there, you will find water." 6. Well, on the next day, Hypatius took all the brothers and went out to the place that had been shown to him. He prayed for a long time together with all the brothers, and as soon as they began to dig, they found water—unadulterated, pure, and quite refreshing. 7. The place was near the chapel, so that the person who drew from the well could run right to the kitchen.

Chapter 20

1. Again, there was another time when worms, horribly, had eaten the grain harvest that the brothers were keeping. Well, knowing that it was already destined for destruction and that nothing could be done, Hypatius filled his sacks and said, "Let's distribute it to the poor along the roadways lest Satan consume it." 2. And so as he went out and gave it to the poor, the Lord also increased the harvest spontaneously without human assistance, and no worm appeared in it any longer; rather, it remained utterly pure.

Chapter 21

1. There was another time when four slaves belonging to the ex-consul Monaxius[1] withdrew [from the world] and came to the monastery, wanting to make their renunciation. [Hypatius] welcomed them and made them monks. 2. Monaxius, however, dispatched [riders] on post-horses[2] with great haste and sought them because one of them was his kinsman; this one he beat severely, even though he had become an extremely well-regarded ascetic and was deemed worthy of the priesthood. 3. After falling heavily on one of them by the name of Paul and torturing him, Monaxius cast him into bondage and handed him over to a soldier to be locked up. 4. During the middle of the night, an angel of God came, loosed his chains, opened the gates, and released him, saying, "Go, and stay safe." 5. Once he was released, and knowing where the others were, he too went to the monastery. For Monaxius had never known about the monastery. 6. After these events, though, he did come to know about it, and, upon learning that his slaves were there, he sent to the saint, saying, "Send me the slaves." 7. But [Hypatius] said to his attendants, "Go and tell him this: 'I am not taking them from God and giving them to you. If you dare to take them, come and take them yourself. For they fled to God.'"

---

[1] A prominent imperial official, who was appointed Urban Prefect of Constantinople (408–409), and Praetorian Prefect of the Orient on two separate occasions (414, 416–420). Based on information presented in this chapter, it seems that he was also consul of the Constantinopolitan senate sometime before his encounter with Hypatius.

[2] The public post was a system established at the beginning of the Roman Empire by Emperor Augustus to ensure that people connected to the imperial administration could travel and communicate swiftly and reliably.

8. But [Monaxius] heard this and was confused at Hypatius's response. He sent priests to exhort him by saying, "Come that I may see you, because I have a longing to see you." 9. Given that he had [already] sent people many times, Hypatius felt compelled to go. Others, though, tried to change Hypatius's mind, saying, "Don't go! He might throw you into prison and demand his people back!" 10. And so Monaxius met with him and became positively ebullient; he swore an oath, saying, "This very night, I saw you praying in my house." 11. Well, he then launched into accusations about the slaves and into a long discourse, that he was well educated and that he had served as prefect three times. "I wish," he said, "that you would send back my slaves." 12. Hypatius, though, as if feigning surprise, said to him, "If you think the thoughts of human beings, naturally they are your slaves; but if you do not think the thoughts of human beings but those of God, then they are not your slaves, but instead fellow slaves.[3] 13. If then you keep them from our common Master, God, what will he do to you? Won't his fire be kindled against you?" 14. Amazed at the man and stricken by his response, [Monaxius] begged him, saying, 15. "Abba, offer a prayer and bless my house and children. Go in peace and pray for me. For no longer will I dare to say that they can't be slaves to God." 16. And so once [Hypatius] prayed for and blessed him, he went back to his monastery.

---

[3] Perhaps a reference to Matt 18:33?

Chapter 22

1. He felt such affection for the needy that he became like a father to orphans and a husband to their mother. Indeed, it is impossible to tell how many naked people he clothed or how many hungry people the Lord nourished through him.[1] 2. Just from his facial expression, one could tell that he loved the poor. 3. God's grace shone in him, according to what's written, "A man's seal is his mercy,"[2] as if the Scripture was fulfilled that said, "Blessed is the one who gives consideration to the poor and needy; on the wicked day, the Lord will rescue him. May the Lord preserve him, give him life, and bless him on the earth."[3] 4. Indeed, no poor person ever left the monastery in need of anything. It is impossible to say how many wounds God treated through him. 5. There were many whom the physicians rejected as being unable to afford treatment because they were [too] poor, and many whom no one could approach because of their stench, and yet it was he who washed away their seropurulent discharge and cared for them with his own hands, using neither a physician nor a salve nor anything else—indeed, he knew nothing of that—but made a paste of boiled lentils and salt, prayed, and made the seal of Christ. In a few days, God supplied the grace, and [Hypatius] discharged them as healthy, whereupon they glorified [God]. 6. To those who had been treated, he commanded them to give thanks not to him, but to God, to glorify him who performed miracles with his slaves.

[1] See Matt 25:31-46.
[2] See Sir 17:22.
[3] See Ps 40:2-3 (41:1-2).

7. How many people who would soon be blind because of white spots [in the eyes] did the Lord cure through him! From among these came someone who could not see and said to Hypatius, "Place the seal upon me, slave of God, and spit into my eyes so that I may open my eyes!" 8. So terribly had he suffered from ophthalmia that he could not open his eyes. 9. And once [Hypatius] prayed and made the seal, immediately the Lord cured him and he went away, able to see.

10. How many people who had been enfeebled by demons did the Lord strengthen through him! Indeed, one time, six men carried one man by the name of Agathangelos,[4] who was thunderstruck when a demon assailed him and brought him [to Hypatius]. 11. [Agathangelos] thrashed and shook all his limbs, and neither his hand nor his foot could stay still. 12. Amidst his screams, his whole body leapt off the ground so that no one could get control of him; rather, the hair of everyone who was watching stood on end from fear, and they spread out their hands to God. 13. Hypatius saw him, made the seal, took him inside, prayed, anointed him with blessed oil, and grabbed three strips of cloth to wrap him up. Within seven days, the Lord cured him.

14. How many people driven mad by demons did the Lord cure through him! So great a gift for healing did he receive from God that he drove out even the most fearsome demons through prayer and the seal of Christ. 15. Indeed, one time, Zoannes the count,[5] who would have become a military commander had he not died, brought to Saint Hypatius his brother by the name of Athelaas,[6] who was being harassed by a terrible demon. 16. The demon, though, was the product of terrible magic. And having filled his hand with gold, the count handed it over to Saint Hypatius, 17. but the latter said to the former, "Did you come [here] to purchase the grace of God for your business? Don't you know that Christ has

---

[4] This person is otherwise unknown.
[5] This person is otherwise unknown.
[6] This person is otherwise unknown.

commanded us, saying, 'You received a gift, so give a gift'?"[7] 18. But the count, who [already] drew immense profit because [Hypatius] had given him guidance without accepting any gold, glorified the God who caused him to meet such a man. 19. The count cleaved to the slave of God as a father until his death. 20. His brother, though, remained in the monastery for a time, and, thanks to the saint's prayer, the Lord identified those who had performed the magic spells and drove the demon out of the man. Once cured, he became healthy, but after Zoannes's death, he became count in his place.

21. Not only were peasants from the regions adjacent to the monastery cured of the evils that befell them, but they would also lead their animals to the saint as soon as they became sick because of either a demon or another misfortune. He would rub the cow's tongue with salt in his hand, pray, and place the seal of Christ on its forehead, and on that very day the Lord would cure it.

[7] Matt 10:8.

Chapter 23

1. Well then, he was sixty years old and became gravely ill, so that we all thought that he was about to die. 2. And finally his disciples, all the poor people, his friends, and outside monks from other monasteries were praying for him and in their grief cried so much that everyone knew that he would gain strength from God on account of their praying and crying. 3. Indeed, after the passing of Saint Dalmatios,[1] everyone then held him as a father. But after his recovery, he told us what happened, saying, "Truly, children, Satan afflicted me by preventing me from going down the good path.[2] 4. For while I was going on my way, the Devil stood up and said, 'Where are you bringing him? I have yet to wrestle with him!' And immediately, my guide said, 'You have yet to contend. So, go back, take heed for your children.'"

[1] See 1.6.
[2] That is, Hypatius wanted to die, but Satan prevented him from doing so.

Chapter 24

1. This, then, is what he always taught us, his disciples, as well as those monks who came from outside the monastery and his friends. I have not forgotten the benefit of his teaching; rather, I recount it [here] so that those who long to learn a spiritual zeal may take up his virtue, and so that all the other brothers who heard his instruction may draw benefit. 2. And so here is what he used to say:

The one who wants to be pleasing to God and to be deemed worthy of the kingdom of heaven must choose the Lord's two commandments, about which he said in the Gospel, 3. "On two commandments hang all the law and prophets," namely, 4. "Love the Lord your God with all your soul, all your mind," and all your strength, and "[Love] your neighbor as yourself."[1] 5. For when the Holy Spirit's compunction first enters into someone, and when it is realized within himself that all the things of this world are vanity[2] and are passing away—"For the present form of this world is passing by"[3]—6. and when he comes to know that he cannot draw profit from it except for when he performs a good deed, [only] once he has gained this [insight] will he take it with him and therefore find mercy from the Lord and finally know that in the world there are many desires distracting him. 7. At that point, he has realized that he must choose to despise the world, go away into his own place, and petition God in tranquility in accordance with

[1] See Matt 22:37-40.
[2] See Eccl 1:14.
[3] 1 Cor 7:31.

the one who said, 8. "Blessed is he who takes up the yoke from his youth; he sits alone, and he will be silent."[4] I wonder (he used to say) whether there is anyone in the world who could blamelessly keep God's commandments by turning away, just as the Lord also said, "No one can be a slave to two lords."[5] 9. It is possible to live in the world with solemnity and righteousness, 10. but greater is he who, because of God, despises all things and has no other concern except for how to please God,[6] petitioning him night and day,[7] just as he said: "Consider your work to be perpetual beseeching."[8] 11. For he who fed six hundred thousand without a seed[9] would not be unable to feed himself. 12. But if [God] comes across reverent men, he will dwell within them. Thus, in time, such a person will learn how to please the Lord from the divine Scriptures, from the instruction of our ancestral holy fathers, and from experience itself. 13. Yes, he must come to know, through the many tribulations and trials with which the Enemy tests him, what the best way to counter the wiles of the Devil is[10] and how sweet a thing it is to cleave to God. 14. Only then, in his soul's strong desire and labor, will he begin to seek and request assistance from him so that, at his coming, the Lord will illuminate his mind and destine him to discern the bitter from the sweet.

15. It is quite a bitter thing to hand oneself over to sin, even though respite seemingly appears in the flesh, and it is quite a sweet thing to traverse the narrow and hard road that brings us to life,[11] where the righteous find respite. 16. Indeed, it has

---

[4] See Lam 3:27-28.

[5] Matt 6:24.

[6] 1 Cor 7:32.

[7] See 1 Thess 3:10.

[8] Quoting either Jesus at Luke 18:1 or Paul at Rom 12:12.

[9] See Exod 12:37 with 16:1-36.

[10] Eph 6:11.

[11] Matt 7:14.

always been the Devil's custom to suggest eating, drinking, wearing different garments, enjoying life, and producing children within a legitimate marriage. 17. But these things are his poisons. Just as a fish is caught on the hook when it eats the bait, so too does the Enemy use these things as bait for us. 18. The married man must yearn for money and, as a result of his yearning for money, commit injustice and swear oaths and quarrel [with competitors], becoming someone who is so preoccupied with business that he does not go to church; finally, he ends up lusting for diverse food and flamboyance in his garments. 19. Because of these things, a darkness and most terrible blindness is born in the soul[12] so that the soul neither finds respite nor seeks God, according to the apostle, who says, "The unmarried person is concerned only for the things of the Lord, how to please him."[13] 20. And if the one who has money keeps acquiring it, let him hear the Lord when he says, "Everyone who leaves home, land, father, mother, brothers, or sisters will receive a hundredfold and inherit eternal life."[14] 21. Let him not be faithless to [the Lord], for [the Lord] is not a liar, and he can give what he promises.[15] For he brought the world into being out of nothing,[16] and he who made you and provided you with money is not incapable of giving it [to you]. 22. "Indeed, no word from God will be powerless";[17] only let us not be faithless, but rather let us hasten to do all things through him. 23. And at that time will we know the works that he did with us, that the affliction, which came because of God, was full of grace and gladness. 24. For if such knowledge of God enters into us, we will not at all be affected by either abuse

---

[12] See Eph 4:18.

[13] 1 Cor 7:32.

[14] Matt 19:29.

[15] See Titus 1:2.

[16] See 2 Macc 7:29.

[17] Luke 1:37.

or hunger or thirst or insult or humiliation or nakedness or persecution or any other affliction,[18] but rather we will remain patient, enduring all things with delight because of God.

25. If we cast all things onto God[19] and do not seek to avenge ourselves,[20] he will make us prosperous in all things[21] and bring about his mercy for us.[22] And just then, in our astonishment, we will know with what kind of master we have sought refuge. 26. For loving God with a whole heart[23] is the same thing as someone in the world being bound by a yearning for a wife or a genuine friend. 27. Even if he is persecuted, even if he is treated with violence, even if he sustains damage, even if he suffers myriad evils, he will not exhaust that love. 28. In this way, the one who yearns for God is always pinned to his love, and despises all the business on earth, and endures every pain while giving thanks to and glorifying God, and hastens always with great yearning to enact his commandments, according to the verse, "You command that your commandments be fervently guarded."[24]

29. Were something unscrupulous to fall upon him, or an affliction, or a war—satanic or human—even if it were possible to become a martyr, he should simply endure all things with grace and not exhaust his love and commandments, according to the Scripture that says, 30. "They brought me close to my end on earth, but I have not forsaken your commandments."[25] He wants to be pleasing to him and to insatiably do all the things that give God respite.

---

[18] See Rom 8:35.
[19] Ps 54:23 (55:22).
[20] See Rom 12:19.
[21] See Ps 1:3.
[22] See Luke 10:37.
[23] See Luke 10:27.
[24] Ps 118(119):4.
[25] Ps 118(119):87.

31. And likewise, too, loving one's neighbor as oneself is the same thing[26] as what the Lord said: "Whatever you would like people to do to you, do the same to them."[27] 32. Whatever good things we would like another person to do to us, let us also do the same for our neighbor, and whatever suffering we would like to avoid from another person, let us also not do that to anyone. 33. This is loving your neighbor in accordance with the Scripture that says, "And he does not do evil to his neighbor,"[28] and, "Love toward your neighbor does not produce evil"[29] but "endures all things."[30] 34. Indeed, see how much God loved us,[31] that, for our sake, a human being was deemed worthy of coming into existence and enduring a cross in order to ransom us from the Devil. He accepts beneficence for the poor and, in exchange for it, offers the kingdom of heaven. 35. "Well then, if God loves us like this, how ought we love each other?"[32]

36. Look at your calling, brothers![33] You were called to an angelic rank! For just as the angels glorify God one by one, so too do you who sing hymns strive to glorify [God] with your works by enacting the virtues, as we said previously—first, love for God and neighbor, then self-control, tranquility, endurance, possessionlessness, prudence, forbearance, and continuous lamentation for sin. 37. The one just starting to taste God's grace howls out, night and day, about how he will please God and traverse the sea of this age, and once he is rescued, he comes into Christ's harbor. 38. And so strive to do these things "so that people may see your good deeds and glorify

[26] See Mark 12:31.
[27] See Matt 7:12.
[28] Ps 14:4 (15:3).
[29] Rom 13:10.
[30] 1 Cor 13:7.
[31] See 1 John 4:9.
[32] 1 John 4:11.
[33] 1 Cor 1:16.

your Father in heaven,"[34] so that the verse "Blessed is that slave" through whom the Lord is glorified[35] also applies to you. 39. As for you who have accepted the angelic life on earth, if you struggle for this short time and, through the grace of Christ, prevail over the wiles of the Enemy[36] and overcome the passions of the flesh and become pleasing to God, you will be far superior to the angels, according to the verse, "Don't you know that we will judge angels?"[37] 40. On the one hand, since they are bodiless, the angels cannot commit sin, but on the other, the flesh itself, which lusts against the Spirit,[38] is our proving-ground. Realize, then, that the righteous will thus shine like the sun[39] and receive ineffable boons. 41. Indeed, it was with reference to you that the Lord said, "You are the salt of the earth. If the salt loses its flavor, how will it regain its saltiness?"[40] 42. Through you, human beings regain their saltiness as they behold your way of life; for you are the world's first fruit.[41] 43. Just as when the farmer threshes the wheat and offers his first fruit to the Lord and, with just a little bit, the Lord blesses all the grain, so too does God show mercy to the world through his saints.

44. Brothers, look at how many boons were given to us, his slaves. First, he liberated us from enslavement to the world[42] and its disturbances, and he brought us who live in tranquility to have no anxiety except how we may make a faultless presentation of our souls to the Lord[43] on the last day and how we may be deemed worthy to stand on his right side.

---

34 Matt 5:16.

35 See Matt 24:46.

36 Eph 6:11.

37 1 Cor 6:3.

38 Gal 5:17.

39 Matt 13:43.

40 Matt 5:13.

41 See Rev 14:4.

42 See Rom 8:21.

43 See 1 Thess 3:13.

45. Second, even though we are unworthy, he allowed us to glorify him night and day and to send up service to him.

46. Third, he furnished us with what [we need] for life, since we did not know [how to acquire it] either through our own hands or through the people who fear him.

47. Fourth, the noble rulers and emperors throughout the world honor us on account of God, something obvious from the fact that they are Christian. 48. For this alone, could we [ever] show the gratitude to the Lord that he deserves? What will we [ever] give back to him in return for all the things that he gave us?[44]

49. Fifth, he deemed us worthy of going from the darkness of ignorance into the light of his knowledge. And why should I say, or why should I mention, that he brought us into being out of nothing? 50. If I would want to enumerate the many boons that he has provided and continues to provide us in this age—for I am unable to speak about the things to come—then "time would run out for me as I recount" them.[45]

51. We were frequently deprived of these things when we were in the world. Sometimes we found ourselves in poverty, and other times we endured hardship, dwelling amidst sins, wars, afflictions, lawcourts, or other things that thrive in the world. And if someone was wealthy, wealth would have [only] supplied further pain to his life.

52. And so, brothers, who is competent to give thanks to God for all these things or to look up exclusively to him? You are blessed who are impoverished in the world and who are rich with God,[46] who have died to the world but live with God[47] in accordance with the verse, "As ones who have nothing and possess all things."[48] 53. "For you died, and your life is

---

[44] Ps 115:3 (116:12).
[45] Heb 11:32.
[46] See Luke 12:21.
[47] See Rom 6:10-11.
[48] 2 Cor 6:10.

hidden with Christ in God."[49] 54. And so, I am saying this to you, my brothers, not only so that we may sing hymns to God when we receive boons from him but also so that, in a similar way, we may run to him in the midst of afflictions and not be separated from him, loving him for everything that happens to us. 55. For oftentimes God is testing us [to see] whether we endure the afflictions [that we suffer] for his love. 56. And so, not just when we are at peace should we be friends of his, and not just when we are in a good and relaxed mood should we be slaves of his and glorify him with psalms and hymns;[50] rather, let us be his slaves when we encounter afflictions, wicked acts, and temptations by eagerly expressing gratitude so that we may be swiftly delivered from temptations. 57. For just as peace provides no nourishment to a soldier, and [just as] he cannot advance to higher distinctions or greater spoils if he does not go to war and fight, so too with the one who loves God: only when he encounters persecutions and torments, and stands before rulers as they subject him to diverse torments in fire, sword, and other tests, does he especially rejoice, endure, and not exhaust his love of God. 58. Indeed he sees in advance the crown that God gives to professional fighters[51] and does not deny his Master or heed any instructions of those who contradict God's will. 59. For the one who has begun to be bound in great love for Christ, "which is the bond of perfection,"[52] sings psalms with his deeds. 60. "What will separate us from the love of Christ? Affliction, confinement, persecution, famine, nakedness, danger, sword,"[53] or any such thing "will not be able to separate us," the faithful, "from the love that is in Christ Jesus, our Lord,"[54] 61. Given

[49] Col 3:3.
[50] See Col 3:16.
[51] See 2 Tim 2:5.
[52] Col 3:14.
[53] Rom 8:35.
[54] Rom 8:39.

that, he has a yearning to testify that it is better for a Christian to endure any of those things for one hour on account of God and be crowned [with martyrdom] than to die in bed with pain. For when the body separates [from the soul], there is great danger and struggle.[55]

62. And so know, children, that self-control is a great possession for a Christian; indeed, it is a bridle for all vices and a spur for all virtues. 63. It tames the body's passions, produces a pure mind, brings one to good knowledge, and sedates the vigor of youth. 64. Fearsome is the battle waged by gluttony, for all vices follow in its wake, and indeed it leads to the body's corruption and the soul's bondage, dragging it down into vice and gaining advantage from the other vices in turn. 65. It takes a plausible appearance, and it argues from Scripture that eating and drinking are not vices: hasn't it been written that it is not what enters a person that causes defilement but rather what comes out?[56] 66. [Gluttony argues that] the Lord spoke those words to the Jews since they accused his disciples of plucking grain on the Sabbath, which was impermissible according to the Law;[57] 67. [the Lord] said to them, "It is not what enters a person that causes defilement," instead of, "May you have also eaten the grain without causing wickedness to grow out of your heart and, while still observing the Sabbath, without angering the creator of the Sabbath!" 68. For our part, we are not stating that self-control is abstinence from all things, but rather that it is the body not drawing nourishment from diverse foods. 69. The vegetable, the legume, and the wheat provide the essentials for life, service to the soul, and energy for good work. 70. Rather, we declare that [self-control] provides direction to the body so that it is not weighed down by foods, so that it does not pull the soul into sin, so that it does

---

[55] The idea here is that the monk who is used to affliction in life will be better prepared to deal with the dangers and struggles that come just after death.

[56] Matt 15:11.

[57] See Matt 12:1-14.

not again oppress the soul, and so that it does not cause it to fall and impede it in spiritual pursuits. 71. The soul ought to treat the body as its slave[58] so that the former may give the latter a small bit when it gets exhausted and intensify [its discipline] when it runs riot again.

72. Excessive food is a spur for many vices in a human being, and self-control is [a spur] for many boons, just as the divine Scriptures teach. 73. At the beginning, our forefather Adam was expelled from Paradise because of food, even though he had everything [there] for his enjoyment.[59] 74. And while they ate manna in the desert, the people wanted[60] Egyptian meat, garlic, onions, leeks, melons, and cucumbers.[61] 75. Once they turned to idols, they angered God, and their legs buckled in the desert.[62] 76. Three children, though, who did not want to be tainted by the idols, requested an exemption from eating at the royal table;[63] by eating seeds, they looked better than those who ate at the king's table, in accordance with the one who said, 77. "I pummel my body and enslave it so that, once I have made my proclamation to others, I myself may not be discredited."[64] 78. And if the great Apostle said this, why shouldn't we say it? "For the athlete is self-controlled in all respects."[65] 79. Should something result from an appetite in his heart, he would make himself an object of derision to his enemies.[66] 80. He who satisfies his stomach cannot fight the mental battle or be released from nocturnal images or bodily pains. 81. "The one who sows for the flesh will reap corruption

---

[58] See 1 Cor 9:27.

[59] See Gen 3:8-23.

[60] See Exod 16:3.

[61] Num 11:5.

[62] Heb 3:17.

[63] Dan 1:7-12.

[64] 1 Cor 9:27.

[65] 1 Cor 9:25.

[66] Sir 18:30-31.

from the flesh, but the one who sows for the spirit will reap eternal life from the Spirit."[67]

82. Do not in turn comport yourself as if you have performed a great feat when you keep self-control or pray or do a good deed, since you know that every boon we have comes from God. 83. "What do you have that you did not receive? And if you did receive it, what is your ground for boasting as if you didn't receive it?"[68] "For unless the Lord builds the house, the builder has toiled in vain";[69] whenever you do everything that has been ordained, then say, "We are worthless slaves; we have done that which we need to do."[70] 85. Yes, the Lord raises in glory[71] those who are humble in mind, and "he gives grace to the humble."[72] On account of our sins, we have done nothing except give ourselves, in some small way, over to the fear of God.

86. Even this comes from God, and, ultimately, he gave us all the other things through his grace. Well, how could we dare to boast that we are righteous or that we have done anything noble? 87. For if someone thinks that he should praise himself, grace will immediately leave him, and what he is becomes manifest, and then he begins to know that he is a human being, full of sins and unable to do something noble except when God's grace comes and dwells within him. 88. Arrogance brings ruin to a person, for "he who exalts himself will be humbled."[73] If someone were to humble his mind and think himself the most insignificant person of all, grace will magnify him. He ought to always keep this in his heart: "The Lord has shown me mercy in this world and has deemed me worthy to

---

[67] Gal 6:18.

[68] 1 Cor 4:7.

[69] Ps 126(127):1.

[70] Luke 17:10.

[71] 1 Cor 15:43.

[72] Prov 3:34.

[73] Luke 14:11.

be his slave." Then [the Lord] by his grace will save him in the age to come. 89. Indeed, no one is made righteous from the works of the Law, in accordance with the verse, "By grace you have been saved."[74] 90. Humility is an unbreakable wall and the crown of all the virtues.

91. And so let us not succumb to acedia[75] in our discipline, but rather let us raise our eagerness to a higher pitch; "forgetting the things that came before and advancing to the things ahead, let us pursue with focus the prize of God's higher calling."[76] 92. Yes, our time is short. Let us hasten to leave for our proper home. 93. "We are strangers and sojourners,"[77] and we have dwelled here for the following reason: with God's help to leave for the cities of the saints and to find repose for the unending ages after we have fought against our foes.

94. And so, let no one be afraid or succumb to acedia by saying, "I must endure so much in my fasting, in my sleeplessness, in my lying on the ground, in my cultivation of discipline in temperance or my battle against demons, that I am weak in body." Rather, by girding himself in faith,[78] let him say, 95. "the God to whom I am a slave provides me with power."[79] For if anyone, with God['s help], prevails in the initial battle, he will become more eager for the next battle.

96. And so, my brothers, hasten to persevere in prayer, "to stay awake and to pray that you may not fall into temptation," just as the Lord said.[80] 97. While you pray, though, "do not let" your mind "be anxious,"[81] but when the mind recovers itself

---

[74] Eph 2:5.

[75] Acedia is a form of listlessness that brings with it boredom, an inability to concentrate, and a sense of purposelessness. It was a frequent concern addressed by monastic writers in late antiquity.

[76] Phil 3:13-14.

[77] Heb 11:13.

[78] See 1 Pet 1:13.

[79] Ps 29:8 (30:7).

[80] Matt 26:41.

[81] Luke 12:29.

from the soul's toil, "let your requests be known to God."[82] 98. And so glorify him night and day amidst "psalms, hymns, and spiritual songs,"[83] in accordance with the Scripture that says, what good does it do if I sing a psalm "in the spirit while my mind is unproductive?"[84] 99. What does this mean? "I will sing psalms with my spirit, but I will also sing psalms in my mind. I will pray in my spirit, but I will also pray in my mind."[85]

100. "Stay sober and stay awake. For your opponent, the Devil, lurks about, looking for someone to devour. Should you who are strong in faith resist him,"[86] he will burn up and flee from you. 101. And so let us not be afraid of the demons, those rogues, our enemies. They are always bragging in our mental images despite having no strength against the faithful; they cannot force us into anything bad, but, using their cunning against us, they can only make, in a speciously artful way, suggestions to us. 102. Finally, once we have utterly purified ourselves, we can invoke the Lord so that he may provide us with the discernment for understanding his arts, in accordance with the verse, "Let us not be ignorant of [the Devil's] ideas."[87] 103. For the Lord's coming has made him weak, and he has no strength against the faithful. Let us not listen to him, then, but rather to the Lord—for our not being persuaded or our being persuaded by him is up to us—and let us not be afraid of his mental images since we have the Lord as our helper. 104. "God did not give us a spirit of cowardice but one of power, love, and willpower."[88]

---

82 Phil 4:6.

83 Eph 5:19.

84 1 Cor 14:14.

85 See 1 Cor 14:15.

86 1 Pet 5:8-9.

87 2 Cor 2:11.

88 2 Tim 1:7.

Chapter 25

1. And so those are the things he taught us, his disciples, at all times. When we heard them from him, though, and saw the miracles that God brought about through him—because the Lord cured many people of various ailments through the imposition of [Hypatius's] hands—we stood in awe and glorified the one who gave such grace to his slaves; our resolution grew, and we knew that this is what God said to him through the voice that entered into him through the air: 2. "I have placed you as a light for the Gentiles to the end of the earth."[1] This is because even when he was alive, his life spurred many people to seek refuge in the light of salvation, to renounce the world and become monks. After he departed to God, his instruction proved profitable to many people and illuminated their path into the light of the Lord.

3. Yes, the light of the Lord is fearing the Lord. Everyone who hears the commandments of the Lord and the instructions of the holy fathers, who keeps his path in the light of the Lord—by performing and keeping God's commandments as well as by humbling himself—has laid his foundation upon rock.[2] [One might object:] "but the rock is Christ."[3] 4. And yet the holy fathers taught us nothing outside of God's commandments.

---

[1] See Isa 49:6; Acts 13:47.
[2] See Matt 7:25.
[3] 1 Cor 10:4.

Chapter 26

1. Saint Hypatius's diet was edible seeds, herbs, and a bit of bread, but in his old age, he partook of a bit of wine. 2. He always ate at the end of the ninth hour,[1] but often he postponed it, and during the forty-day fast[2] he ate every other day while cloistering himself, singing, and praying Lauds, Terce, Sext, None, Vespers, Compline, and Matins, in accordance with the one who said, "Seven times a day I praised you for the judgments of your righteousness."[3] He did this during each twenty-four-hour period, singing seven times one hundred psalms and one hundred prayers. Enacting this regimen until his death, he bequeathed it to his disciples, but even in his old age, he did not relent in the diet to which he held. 4. For he always remained healthy, his body held strong, and his face was so fresh that [it looked] as if he partook of extravagant provisions. 5. For truly, the saints partake of noble provisions when they derive enjoyment at the divine and spiritual table within the inner person.

[1] Just before four o'clock.

[2] That is, Lent.

[3] Ps 118(119):164. Callinicus lists the monastic schedule of prayers: the dawn prayer (Lauds at 6 a.m.), the third-hour prayer (Terce at 9 a.m.), the sixth-hour prayer (Sext at 12 p.m.), the ninth-hour prayer (None at 3 p.m.), the sunset prayer (Vespers at 6 p.m.), the late-evening prayer (Compline at 9 p.m.), and the midnight prayer (Matins at 12 a.m.).

Chapter 27

1. While he prayed, he possessed ceaseless compunction, and he wept and cried out to God so much that we remained afraid while shedding [our own] tears. 2. He used to always say to us, "The monk has this foundation for progress: renouncing his own intentions, fulfilling obedience to his spiritual father, and casting every concern and hope on God because he is concerned for our affairs. 3. For the Lord does not neglect those who place their hopes in him. Look, after you dismissed the world and your parents on account of God, you came to my lowly station and entrusted the burden of your lifestyle to me. Well then, you should do what I tell you. 4. For I too try to say what is pleasing to God. As for you, then, listen to me so that we are both pleasing to God and I may be deemed worthy to say with you on that day, 5. 'Look, God, here I am, and here are the children that you gave to me!'" 6. And so, while teaching us these things, he wrote other instructions on a sheet of papyrus and passed it down so that, through these words, we may be pleasing to the Lord.[1] 7. To friends who came to the monastery, he spoke about their obligations, that they might not prefer anything to the fear of God, that they should flee the unrighteous, that they should continuously exert themselves for the churches and act mercifully as much as they could. 8. And so, instructed with these words, they would embrace him and leave, all the better for it.

---

[1] The text does not survive. It is possible that Callinicus is using it, or at least appealing to its existence, as the source for much of the material in Hypatius's extended discourses throughout the *Life*.

Chapter 28

1. Once, when a layperson with a terrible ulcer—indeed, his entire thigh was decaying—approached him, [Hypatius] took care of him by praying for him, and yet no improvement came to the person. 2. At that point, Saint Hypatius said to him, "What act of wickedness have you committed?" He responded, "Before I came to the monastery, a dagger-wielding woman uttered charms over my ulcer." 3. So, after he made this confession, Saint Hypatius told us the story of [what happened next], saying, "During that very night, I saw the woman sitting outside the gate and the Devil sitting just a little distance from her under a canopy, in the form of an imperial official, with an entourage of many demons. 4. The brothers ran out to chase the woman, and the demons wrestled with the brothers. 5. But when I got there, the Devil said to his servants, 'Give him room! You can't do anything against him.' 6. And immediately the Lord made all of them disappear." And the person became healthy within a few days.

7. Once again, they brought to him another person, whose head was so swollen that whoever saw the mass [would think that] three heads had become one; it also had an ulcer on it. 8. But he was servant of a dromikos, as some call the horse-groomer. So, after [Hypatius] prayed and washed his hands, he took care of him. 9. After a considerable number of days, Hypatius was surprised that his suffering was increasing; he said to the man, "Confess! What have you done to offend God? God would not make our efforts fail without a reason." 10. After he refused to confess, the slave of God saw five demons in the night saying to him, "Why do you want to take the man from us? Stop it! He has been handed over to us because of his lawlessness." 11. The saint responded,

"What kind?" They said, "He is married, but he committed adultery with the wife of another; after the adulterous act, he swore an oath on the Gospel; after he swore the oath, he went and had communion in the morning." 12. After that, the saint said to the man, "Did you do this?" He answered in the affirmative. Then he said to him, "When I asked you earlier, you failed to confess. Look, you've got three days left, and then you will die. 13. If you had proclaimed it and repented, we too would have implored God to forgive and heal you." Eventually, the man lost hope and died three days later. "For the soul that sins will die."[1]

14. Another time, again, some monks had a very little church three mile markers away. And a magician came to them under the pretense of making a renunciation. He had a little boy with him. 15. There [the boy] remained, tormenting the brothers and the head of the monastery on certain occasions. The head of the monastery was called Eumathius, a wonderful man, filled with love for God.[2] He sent for Hypatius, imploring him to come to him because he was completely tormented. 16. As soon as he left to see, [Hypatius] knew right away who the man was. 17. It happened that the child had made a mistake there, and [the man] got covered in blood from beating the child. Hypatius took the rod with which the man had beaten the child and bludgeoned [the man], saying, "Did you come here to commit murder?" 18. [The man] became incensed and issued a threat, saying, "Within one week, I will get to exact my vengeance on you." 19. Well, Hypatius went to his own monastery, and, after five days, he saw four demons in the form of camels, but with dragons' necks and heads. 20. But God's angel appeared just above him and picked him up. The demons stuck out their necks to get hold of him, but they were unable [to get him] because he went up higher. 21. Finally the angel showed him the man lying under his bed in the form of a slave[3] with his hair anointed and

---

[1] Ezek 18:4.

[2] This monk is otherwise unknown.

[3] That is, a slave of God, or monk.

said, "He sent them." 22. Hypatius said to the demons, "To you demons, I speak in the name of my Lord, Jesus Christ! The one who sent you to deal with me, go and deal with him in the same way!" 23. Immediately, they turned toward the one who sent them, and he was suddenly overcome and recklessly began to devour his own tongue and hands. 24. Yet again, the brothers came to Hypatius and said, "It's horrifying! He is eating himself up, and he invoked your name! Deign to come and pray on his behalf!" 25. It happened that Hypatius was cloistered—for Lent had come—and he answered them, "Let him be punished for a bit so that he may come to know the fear of God. Then, give him respite at holy Easter." 26. So when he finished his fast on holy Easter, Saint Hypatius left, found him in dreadful circumstances, and said to him, " 'Is God unjust by inflicting his wrath? I'm speaking like a human being. Certainly not!'[4] 27. Don't you know that God shields his slaves?" And immediately he prayed on [the man's] behalf, anointed him with oil, and made the seal of Christ. 28. Immediately, the Lord healed him from the Wicked One, but [the man] was unable to stand because of the extremity of his self-harm. 29. Then Hypatius said to Abba Eumathius, "Within a few days, he'll regain his health, and you should release him thereafter." 30. And the brothers who were rescued from that affliction gave thanks to God.

31. Again, another person, a lector of the holy apostles,[5] got married near the monastery; he received half the dowry and asked the bride's parents for the other half. The bride was not getting pregnant. 32. However, the bride's parents had grown angry with her even before the wedding, and when they realized that she was not getting pregnant, they not only refused to pay the full dowry but also had no intention of making peace with their daughter. Both came to Hypatius, and the bride asked to make peace with her parents. 33. Hypatius said, "Make peace with your daughter." They refused, saying, "If she dies, we should get [back] what we

---

[4] Rom 3:5-6.
[5] Presumably referring to the church at the Rufinianae.

gave for the dowry since they would not have produced a child." 34. Well, some time passed and they had no intention of making peace with their daughter, and so Hypatius finally called the bride in front of everyone, and standing there out in the open, he said, 35. "I say to you in the name of our Lord Jesus Christ, you will get pregnant and give birth to a son and you will name him Personas after his grandfather." 36. And after she became pregnant, she gave birth and named him Personas, with God putting the word of his slave into action. 37. "For he puts the will of those who fear him into action and responds to their petition."[6] And in accordance with the law, [the bride's parents] paid back what was owed and made peace [with their daughter] and glorified God for what had happened.

38. Another time, a peasant came to the slave of God by the name of Zeno;[7] he was laid so low by a demon that he did not know where he was. He was muttering gibberish and assailing everyone. 39. His village, though, was six mile markers from the monastery. Weeping, his wife fell before the holy Hypatius. 40. But Hypatius said to everyone, "The Lord spoke to the blind man, 'Do you believe that I can do this?'[8] 41. Well, if the Lord asks for faith from the one who comes to him, how much more [faith] ought we sinful human beings [have]. 42. If you have faith in my God, to whom I have been a slave since my youth, that he will provide the healing to you through my intercession, then God will readily give you the treatment. 43. So if those who make offerings do not have some faith, the intercessor cannot easily be heard, since the faith of the one who comes to prayer is not cooperating.[9] 44. So if his faith cooperates with the prayer, God will heal the one who makes the prayer and bestow remedies. 45. For no one thinks that a person can in any way be healed without the grace of God, just as the Lord

---

[6] Ps 144(145):19.

[7] This person is otherwise unknown.

[8] Matt 9:28.

[9] See Jas 2:22.

said, 'Treat the sick, cast out demons! Having received a gift, give it out.'[10] 46. It is clear that the worthy receive the gift of healings from God, and, when it cooperates with them, it bestows cures."

47. With these words, he instructed those who came to him for treatment so that they would glorify God, who saves those who glorify him and who cures every disease through the intercession of his saints. 48. So after receiving Zeno, [Hypatius] secured [Zeno's] hands by covering him with a sleeveless sackcloth so that he was restrained and his hands were secure inside. 49. The sackcloth was incredibly strong, for he used that very sackcloth to cover those dreadful demoniacs who rushed up to people in order to strike them, and they would not rush up to anyone; rather, by remaining steady in fasting and prayer, they became docile. 50. For God healed them through the saint's intercession. So Zeno, amidst his gibberish, spoke to the slave of God thus: 51. "What do you have to do with me, human? Why are you taking away what is mine? I am bringing them together, and you are wickedly scattering them.[11] What do you have to do with me? Why are you plundering my possessions? What do you have to do with me?"[12] 52. When they heard these words, the brothers smiled and rejoiced at once; they sang hymns to God and were eager to become genuine slaves to God, seeing the miracles that God wrought through those that fear him. 53. Within a few days, then, [God] healed him. [Zeno] went back to his own house, but immediately wandered into the disarray of his [former] lifestyle; the impure spirit again returned to him.[13] 54. Again, they brought him back to the monastery, and [his condition] had grown worse than it was at first since he did not take any food. 55. When the saint came, he fed him by hand, and [Zeno] took it with difficulty. And so after he remained there for a bit of time and became healed, yet again he was abused [by

---

[10] See Matt 10:28.
[11] See Matt 12:30.
[12] Matt 8:29.
[13] See Matt 12:43-44.

the demon], and they brought him [back] for a long time. And then they brought him back for a fourth time. 56. Finally, the Lord healed him, and [Zeno] gave thanks to Saint Hypatius, glorifying God. From there on out, he remained healthy. 57. The saint was very long-suffering and had deep compassion for those subject to the passions. He used to say, "Is this the one whom those bandits, the demons,[14] thrash? Is he half-dead? Let us render mercy to him on account of God, for when the Lord came, he redeemed Adam through the baptism in which those who have faith in him are baptized."

[14] See Luke 10:30.

Chapter 29

1. Saint Hypatius used to read quietly, for he possessed a yearning for the divine Scriptures and ardently cherished any canonical book he came across that presented a system for [cultivating] moral character.[1] He rarely came out except to [visit] the nearby apostolic church each Sunday for God's liturgy, and after its conclusion, he went straight back to the monastery. 2. Such was his sagacity that he was always regarded as possessed by God. Indeed, he was clairvoyant with respect to events, and, through the grace of God, he foresaw outcomes. 3. For some of the scholastici[2] who had made their renunciations had become his disciples, and if ever, with the skill of their education, they wanted to play the philosopher in conversation, he would immediately speak with them [to see] whether they answered rightly according to justice or with the artifice of philosophy.

[1] What Callinicus has in mind here is uncertain, but it seems to be non-biblical literature, such as apostolic acts, accounts of martyrs, or even hagiographies.

[2] See 1.1, with the note.

Chapter 30

1. He possessed a zeal for God and purged many places in the Bithynian region of idolatrous error. For if he heard of a place where some people were worshiping either a tree or something else like that, then he would immediately go there with his monastic disciples in tow; after cutting it down, he would burn it in the fire. And thus, little by little, they finally became Christians. 2. For this is also how Lord Jonah, who had been his father, purged Thrace and made Christians. 3. But as for Saint Hypatius, if he saw a place where someone[1] was disregarding his work for God, he would be moved by zeal and say to us,

4. Children, focus on the work of God lest I become irritated. For in my irritation, I do not regard my prayer as pure. 5. Likewise, it is a good thing to have a little discomfort so that we know that we are human sinners, just as the Apostle says: 6. "A thorn in the flesh was given to me, a messenger of Satan, so that I would be discomforted lest I become arrogant."[2] 7. From the point when God ordered me to guide you, his flock, he set over me a punishment if I failed to preach the Gospel and teach you the path of God. 8. Yes, I am wary lest I get rebuked like Eli, because he did not penalize for the purpose of correction his own sons, the priests Hophni and Phinehas. He received wrath along with them.[3] 9. For the apostle said, "Rebuke, penalize, exhort,"[4] and, "One who loves

---

[1] Presumably a monk.
[2] 2 Cor 12:7.
[3] See 1 Sam 2:12-36.
[4] 2 Tim 4:2.

his son will discipline him."[5] 10. As for you, children, focus on erecting virtue while God furnishes you with grace and endurance; when your heart is unwilling, throttle it with violence toward a good end, "in all endurance and patience."[6] 11. "Abstain from every form of wickedness; testing all things, hold fast to the good."[7] 12. "For you need endurance so that when you perform the Lord's will, you preserve the promise."[8] For the kingdom of heaven belongs to the violent, and the violent take it by force.[9]

[5] Heb 12:5, quoting Prov 3:12.
[6] Col 1:11.
[7] 1 Thess 5:21-22, but with clauses reversed.
[8] Heb 10:36.
[9] See Matt 11:12.

Chapter 31

1. He performed such great acts of mercy for the poor and needy monks that onlookers glorified God and said, 2. "Truly this man is Christ's highest in accordance with his name,[1] and Christ gives abundantly to him." 3. Indeed, once there was a famine about to strike, and, in the night, [Hypatius] saw himself giving bread to the poor, and God's angel, ever present with him, said to him, 4. "Keep guard, Abba, for a famine must strike so that you may then give to them too." And the very next day, he summoned his friend, borrowed some seed and bread at a fair interest rate, and then laid some aside. Within ten days, scarcity struck so that one could not find even half the [regular] merchandise for sale then. And famine prevailed for three years. 5. The entirety of the rural population was famine-struck, and they had to rely on God and [Hypatius], especially during the winters. 6. The venerable one, though, bade them to boil the seed and to gather approximately five hundred souls at the ninth hour. While everyone was eating, he said the "Lord Have Mercy," and, with gratitude and prayer, they took nourishment throughout the day so that the Scripture was fulfilled, 7. "He scattered [the seed] and gave to the poor; his righteousness remains for ever and ever; his horn will be exalted in glory."[2] 8. And just as [it is written] in another place, "The whole world of possessions belongs to the faithful, but not even an obol belongs to the faithless."[3]

---

[1] A play on Hypatius's name: "highest" in Greek is *hýpatos.*
[2] Ps 111(112):9.
[3] Prov 17:6 (LXX).

9. If anyone back then drew some profit for his own life and wanted to pronounce him as blessed to his face, [Hypatius] would show disgust and say to him, 10. "If you saw anything good, brother, it was God's. If you saw anything else, that was mine. Glorify God, then, and give thanks to him. Do not pronounce a man blessed before his death.[4] 11. For so long as we are in this flesh, we are subject to the fear and trembling that, as human beings, we stumble and offend God. 12. Until the final day, then, no one may boast or be free from anxiety; rather, we are obliged to work out our own salvation with fear and trembling, having God as our co-worker."[5]

13. If, then, any extremely rich person, or a wise person, or a lover of God wanted to build a martyrium on their lands, that person would pray for [Hypatius] to make some of his disciples into clerics [for the shrines], saying, "They are truly the crucified ones."[6] 14. And many people entreated him to supply them, but he would not do so easily.

---

[4] See Sir 11:2, 30.
[5] See Phil 2:12-13.
[6] See Gal 6:14.

Chapter 32

1. In those [days], when Nestorius[1] was coming from Antioch and was about to become bishop in the luminous city of Constantine[2]—escorted by Dionysius,[3] the commander who came from the west—2. just as he was approaching the city's suburbs, Saint Hypatius saw [in a vision] that in the holy church of the megalopolis itself there were some laypersons installing [Nestorius] on the [episcopal] throne, and immediately a voice spoke: "Three seasons and half a season, and the weed will be ripped out." 3. So Hypatius began to say to certain people and to the brothers, "I am wary, children, because of what's going to happen, because I've had a vision about him, that he will pervert the faith and that he'll rule for three and a half years." 4. So, around that time, when Nestorius heard (I don't know from where) that he would be passing through the monastery, he did not want to come for a meeting with the saint, as he had arranged with everyone everywhere along his travels. 5. So when he entered the megalopolis and became bishop, he immediately sent clergy members to Hypatius, telling

[1] Bishop of Constantinople, 429–431. He had previously been a monk and priest in Antioch. His dyophysite Christology and controversial disapproval of venerating the Virgin Mary as *theótokos* ("God-bearer") spurred a highly politicized conflict with Cyril of Alexandria, which in turn spurred several centuries of conflict involving clergy, monks, and government officials throughout the eastern Roman Empire.

[2] That is, Constantinople.

[3] A well-documented imperial official who had several high-ranking posts. See J. R. Martindale, *The Prosopography of the Later Roman Empire, Volume II: A.D. 395–527* (Cambridge: Cambridge University Press, 1980), 365–66, Flavius Dionysius 13.

them, 6. "Once you have left, tell that dreamer,[4] 'I'll have twenty years to rule over the city. Where are your dreams [now]?'" 7. Hypatius said to them, "Tell the bishop, 'If what I've seen comes to pass, it was a revelation; if not, it was a dream, and I was simply deluded like a human being.'" 8. So, confused at this response that had been sent, [Nestorius] again sent some other people after a bit of time to seize upon certain words of his. Those who tested him with inappropriate and useless interrogations not only found no words to seize upon but were also surprised and retreated once they realized his great intelligence. From them on, Nestorius kept quiet and no longer sent anyone to him. 9. At the end of the three years, the wicked man gradually began to reveal what he had stored in his heart.[5] 10. For while giving a sermon, he uttered unspeakable things about the Lord—it would not be dignified to repeat them— things that would come back to haunt him.[6] The wretched man was unaware of the divine Scripture that says, "Who will describe this generation?"[7] and, "Don't scrutinize things that are deeper than you."[8] 11. But when Hypatius realized that Nestorius had thoughts that were contrary to what one should have, Hypatius immediately removed his name in the apostolic church so that he would not be referenced in the offering.[9]

12. Now, when the most pious bishop Eulalius[10] learned of this, fearing the emergence of a lawsuit because [Nestorius] would have grounds for it, the latter made it clear to the former that he should rebuke Hypatius. For Nestorius still held power in the city. 13. So

---

[4] See Gen 37:19.

[5] Luke 6:45.

[6] Literally, "he uttered unspeakable things about the Lord . . . against his own head."

[7] Isa 53:8.

[8] See Sir 3:21.

[9] That is, Hypatius removed Nestorius's name from the diptychs, which would be a public sign of disapproval.

[10] Bishop of Chalcedon, a suburb of Constantinople not far from the Rufini-anae.

Eulalius spoke to Hypatius like this: "Why did you remove his name without thinking about the consequence?" 14. Hypatius responded, "For my part, as soon as I realized that he was uttering injustices about my Lord, I stopped having communion with him and referencing his name. For he is not a bishop." 15. At that point, the bishop [Eulalius] angrily said, "Go and fix what you did, for I have the right to take action against you!" 16. But Hypatius answered, "Do what you want. For my part, I chose to suffer all things, and I acted accordingly." 17. So when Nestorius was traveling to Ephesus and a synod was being organized,[11] on the day when he was about to be deposed, Hypatius saw an angel of the Lord exercising power and bringing the holy apostle John[12] to the most pious emperor, saying, 18. "Tell the emperor, 'Give your judgment to Nestorius.'" And after hearing him, he gave it. 19. And he noted the day, and it was discovered that the very day of his deposition was when the three and a half years had been finished, just as the Lord had indicated to him in advance.[13] 20. And after a few days, the deposition of Nestorius was brought forth and read before all the clergy and people, while Eulalius and Hypatius were present in the church.

---

[11] The Council of Ephesus in 431. Nestorius's rival, Cyril of Alexandria, choreographed the proceedings so that Nestorius would be deposed.

[12] John was believed to be the apostolic originator of the episcopal line of succession at Ephesus. A magnificent basilica was built there that housed his relics.

[13] Nestorius was deposed at the Council of Ephesus on June 22, 431.

Chapter 33

1. Again, at another time, the prefect Leontius[1] tried to revive the Olympic games in Chalcedon's theater, games that former emperors and Constantine, worthy of eternal memory, had terminated. 2. So, when Hypatius heard about this, he expressed so extreme an outpouring of zeal that he moaned, wept, shouted up to God, and said, "My Lord, does this mean that idolatry should flourish while I am alive? Don't allow it, Master!" 3. And immediately he said to the brothers, "If anyone is frightened of dying for Christ, then don't come with me." 4. Approximately twenty brothers followed him, and they went straight to Bishop Eulalius. 5. While the bishop was mulling over his jurisdiction, [Hypatius] said to him, "I heard about this, and I know that idolatry is on the verge of approaching us and God's holy church at the Olympic games. I've decided to die in the theater rather than allow this to happen."

6. But at this, the bishop stood up and said to him, 7. "You would prefer to simply die even though no one is compelling us to sacrifice? You're a monk: sit down and shut up![2] This matter rests with me." 8. But [Hypatius] responded, "Since the matter rests with you and you don't care, and since I'm seeing [both] the Master being dishonored by those attempting [to do] this and the Christian people going about in ignorance and committing idolatry, I've

---

[1] A well-documented imperial official who was prefect of the city of Constantinople in 434–435. See Martindale, *Prosopography of the Later Roman Empire*, 669, Leontius 9.

[2] It appears that Eulalius is mocking Hypatius here: "shut up" renders the Greek *hēsýchaze*, a term frequently used in this text and other monastic literature to indicate ascetic tranquility.

come to testify to Your Holiness that tomorrow, when the prefect takes his seat, I will have to enter with a crowd of monks and pull the prefect down from on high. That's how I will die for Christ rather than allow this to happen while I am alive."

9. But the bishop, even in other matters, often treated [Hypatius] with insolence and contempt. But Hypatius went straight to the archimandrites [in the region], saying, 10. "Come fight alongside me so that we persecute the Devil. But if we lose, let us die for Christ." All of them rejoiced and obeyed him as their father. 11. When Leontius realized that the monks had agreed to block him [from reviving the games], he feigned illness and crossed the river back to Constantinople, doing none of the things that he had wanted to do. 12. For when Hypatius wanted to play the athlete, the Lord refuted the will of those who had set their minds on evil things. 13. But from this occasion and from many others too, realizing that Hypatius had been crucified,[3] and that he did all things for God, and that God made him prosper, Bishop Eulalius very much paid him the utmost honor and showed him respect almost like that to a father. For he was living a completely reverent, utterly solemn, and upright life. 14. But Hypatius showed so much zeal for the Olympic games affair that it was a struggle for him to even learn about it and what the wickedness of this practice was. For he only had partial knowledge about it, and that from hearsay. 15. And so, as he was worrying about it, God sent to him a man by the name of Eusebius,[4] who knew all about it. 16. So this Eusebius said that the Olympic games were a wholly dreadful festival belonging to Satan, that it was completely filled with idolmania, and that it would bring ruin and destruction to Christians. And he set this account out for him in a document.

---

[3] Perhaps a reference to Luke 9:24-25 or Gal 5:24. The sense seems to be that Hypatius has mortified his flesh and died to the world.

[4] This person is otherwise unknown.

Chapter 34

1. The blessed one used to evince such possessionlessness and indifference to riches that he persuaded us by often saying, "I have never had in my heart, 'What have I ever acquired in this world?' but [only], 'God appointed me a steward.'" 2. In those days, a scholasticus[1] left him an inheritance of a few coins and garments, and immediately [Hypatius] gave the coins to the monasteries and the garments to the poor. A few of the garments, though, still remained. 3. He said to the brother who stood next to him, "Go, lay them out so that they're not eaten by moths." 4. After he shook them out, the brother said to Abba Hypatius, "Bid me to bind them with some fabric so that they don't get eaten." 5. But Hypatius rebuked him by saying, "You deserve a rebuke for saying, 'I will bind them for storage,' instead of, 'I am giving them to the poor.'" 6. The brother drew great profit from seeing his love for the poor.

[1] See 1.1, with the note.

Chapter 35

1. A[nother] scholasticus,[1] who heard about Saint Hypatius and who was completely Christian, was known to him and was a heartfelt friend to him. Yes, he yearned for God and honored reverent men. 2. He also had three other brothers, and they were likewise scholastici. Of them, though, two had not yet received baptism. 3. Knowing in his mind that Hypatius was greatest in the love for God and that he was adorned with faith and virtue,[2] he went out and brought his brothers. 4. They spoke to Abba Hypatius and put him to the test: "A virgin, a free woman, wants to take a guestroom and stay with you tomorrow." 5. But Abba Hypatius, who knew everything through God's grace, said to them, "There is a guestroom, and we are receiving."

6. Hypatius was not one to meet with a woman casually. And they said to him, "If Your Holiness were to receive us, we would be willing to take the holy baptism so long as God furnishes it through your hands." 7. For they drew immense benefit from his instruction, having also heard about his life from their aforementioned brother. 8. And so, immediately, Hypatius gave thanks to the Lord and gave them his lesson; he said, "Children, focus on saving your souls[3] on a daily basis, because this is the [only] gain you will keep from the world. Everything else remains here." 9. You see, they were quite rich and lived sumptuously.

10. And so, when he baptized them, the grace of God was poured out[4] on one of them to such a degree that bystanders

---

[1] See 1.1, with the note.
[2] See 3 Macc 6:1.
[3] See Mark 8:35.
[4] See Ps 44:3 (45:2).

thought that his soul was caught up into heaven.[5] 11. Before he had consented to be baptized, he used to boast about how he conducted life's affairs. 12. But at the moment of his baptism, God filled him with so much compunction that he immediately renounced all the world's affairs and had no other concern except how to be pleasing to God. 13. Praying and weeping night and day, he brought us to compunction. He humbled his thought and considered himself last of all people.[6] 14. And Saint Hypatius loved him, and, seeing the change wrought by the Holy Spirit, he wanted to keep [the man] near himself, but [the man] said that he was going away to save his wife too. 15. Hypatius told him, "If you go back, they'll immediately ordain you a priest." And it happened just as he had told him: [the man] was ordained with his wife, and they continued to live together with each other in a holy way as two brothers.[7] 16. And emulating Saint Hypatius's lifestyle, he lived in a reverent way so that all drew profit from him; intending to imitate the Abba, and moved by longing, he requested that the *Life* of the Abba be written.[8] 17. After a bit of time, his brother[9] was deemed worthy of [becoming] a priest too, and living with singular purpose, they became fervent slaves to God.

[5] See 2 Cor 12:4.

[6] See Mark 9:35.

[7] The Greek mentions that the man was ordained a priest, but the phrasing suggests that his wife was also ordained.

[8] This sentence suggests that the very idea for the *Life of Hypatius* came from this scholasticus. For further discussion, see the introduction to this volume.

[9] Presumably the other brother who had not received baptism, mentioned at the beginning of this chapter.

Chapter 36

1. How many others too, as soon as they saw Hypatius, were possessed of a yearning to be baptized by his hands? 2. How many from the heresies and the Hellenes converted? How many became monks and came to despise the world? 3. How many, storm-tossed amidst quotidian affairs, sought refuge with God and with him, and got help? Indeed, his fame went everywhere and was heard by all. 4. Did any foreigner come to him and not receive respite? Or did any distressed person not receive consolation? 5. Yes, he suffered with those who suffered and offered encouragement to those who had become discouraged in their discipline. Upon seeing that he had grown old and [still] fought as he did, all took encouragement. 6. With regard to the wounded, lame, blind, paralyzed, or ill, the Lord healed so many of them through his prayers that it would not be possible to narrate each one of their stories.

7. But when they heard about him in the East and in the West, they wrote to him as if to a father and sent blessings to him from Jerusalem, Egypt, Syria, Rome, Asia, and Thessalonica. 8. All the archimandrites, bishops, and reverent men from the desert prayed that they might receive written responses and blessings from him. He did send written responses, exhorting all of them to pray on his behalf so that, he would say, "we may pass through this age happily."

Chapter 37

1. The most pious emperor Theodosius, visiting him for the second time, embraced him and saluted him, saying, "Just as I heard, so I also see." 2. [Theodosius] frequently wrote [to Hypatius] as though to a father and exhorted him to write him back; [Hypatius] wrote him back this prayer as though to a Christian: "May the Lord give you to find in your immaculate heart[1] his righteous decrees."[2] 3. Three empresses—[that is,] three sisters of the emperor—yearned to see Hypatius and approached the apostolic church, to [Rufinus's] palace, and plainly stated to him, "Come out so that we may see you, or let us come to you so that we may be blessed!" 4. He went out, constrained to do so because they loved Christ; he gave them the benefit of his instruction, and, after performing a prayer, he blessed them, and they withdrew.

[1] 1 Chr 28:9.
[2] Ps 118:94 (LXX).

Chapter 38

1. Two other scholastici[1] were known to [Hypatius], and they frequently paid him visits as if to a father, amazed at his understanding and lifestyle. 2. They described to us how they saw God's many miracles in the man. 3. Some of them also told us this: "We returned to our region, but our little slave child poked his eye with a stick so that chunks of flesh, along with his eye, were dangling to the point that they nearly fell off. Amidst everyone's screams, we didn't know what to do. 4. One of them, though, a fellow slave, said, 'Get a blessing from Saint Hypatius! His eye may yet be healed!' 5. After they sent some messengers and received a blessing from the saint, they returned; after rinsing his eye with water, they bandaged it; after unwrapping it on the next day, they found it back to normal and healthy, just like his other eye—and everyone glorified God."

6. And others often described how the Lord saved them through the blessings of Saint Hypatius when they found themselves far away and besieged by dangers. 7. There was once a person who had been shipwrecked and rescued with [some other] people—all the ship's cargo was lost—but two of the sailors got their hands on containers of silk and asked whose they were. 8. The person then said, "Open them up, and if blessings of Saint Hypatius are found, they're mine." 9. After opening them up, they thus discovered [the blessings], and they glorified God because they had not gotten wet except for one garment.[2]

---

[1] See 1.1, with the note.

[2] The "blessings" here probably refer to written blessings that were placed with the silk to keep them safe from sea dangers.

10. There was a stable next to the monastery where horses for the public post[3] were kept, and a demon entered it and killed the horses. The stable keeper went [out] crying and fell before Saint Hypatius. 11. The one gave the other some water, which he blessed, saying, "Sprinkle it in the building and on the horses." [Hypatius] gave it to him and uttered a blessing; [he told him], "Hang [the written blessing] in your building and the demon will flee." 12. Well, he left and did as the saint told him, and no longer did any animal die, because the demon had run away.

13. A home-invading demon used to terribly afflict many peasants by killing either a cow or sheep. 14. Some of the peasants went directly to [Hypatius] crying for him to go out and perform a prayer. And when he went out and performed the prayer, the Lord healed [the animals].

---

[3] Or "racetrack." The Greek *drómou* bears either meaning, and the monastery was close enough to Constantinople that is possible that racehorses were quartered just outside the city.

Chapter 39

1. Long after Nestorius had been driven away,[1] high-ranking officials, clergy members, and reverent ascetics often came to [Hypatius] and asked him whether Nestorius could return to the city of Constantine. 2. This is what he said to them:

> If it is time for the Antichrist, then Nestorius must return to the city of Constantine, but if it is not time for the Antichrist, then neither is it time for Nestorius to return to the city of Constantine. 3. For Nestorius's teaching lays the groundwork for the Antichrist. 4. Really, brothers, I get inflamed at the impiety of those who utter his words and who think his incomprehensible thoughts. "Bold, willful"[2]—speculating about what they haven't seen[3]—that's what Nestorius and his partisans are; God's wrath homes in on them,[4] and "their destruction won't be asleep,"[5] unless they turn back and repent of their lawless deceit.[6] 5. Would that we are able to walk with the eyes of our mind illuminated[7] upon the true path and keep

[1] Nestorius never returned to Constantinople after leaving the imperial capital for Ephesus in May 431. In September 431 the deposed Nestorius returned to his monastery in Antioch before being sent into exile, first to Petra and then to the Great Oasis in the Egyptian desert.

[2] 2 Pet 2:10.

[3] Col 2:18. This is probably the sense, but the Greek is strange here, causing several biblical translations to include a note that the meaning is unclear in Colossians.

[4] See Bar 2:9.

[5] 2 Pet 2:3.

[6] See Acts 3:19?

[7] Eph 1:18.

the faith that the apostles handed down for us, worshiping one God in three hypostases! 6. One will, one power, one divinity, one kingdom of the Father, Son, and Holy Spirit, and the true humanification of the Only-Begotten, who was given flesh from the Holy Spirit and the Virgin Mary in accordance with the pious tradition of the fathers, and who was seen by us in the flesh, and who worked divine wonders and miracles, and who, in his flesh, suffered the cross and death on our behalf, and has raised us, who had been broken down by sin, together with himself and guides us up to the primal blessedness.

7. His listeners rejoiced and embraced him at being taught so well.

Chapter 40

1. One time, when he went out on a Sunday to [the church of] the Holy Apostles, a foreign woman was found yelling and treating herself contemptuously;[1] she adjured him and said, 2. "What do you have to do with me,[2] Hypatius? Don't torment me!" 3. And she went up to the doorstep [of the church] and remained there, mangling herself to the point of harm. Immediately, he went out and sealed her by performing a prayer. 4. But she fell to his feet, and, after keeping silent for one moment, she stood up, having come to her senses: God had provided a healing to her through the imposition of the saint's hands.

5. Another person, a young man by the name of Alexander,[3] was brought by his own father, who was crying and petitioning the saint about his son. 6. [Hypatius] said, "Let him remain at the monastery." 7. He remained there for forty days, and the demon kept dwelling in him, reluctant to get out. Finally, once the saint prayed, the demon left, screaming loudly.

8. Again, there was a young man by the name of Stephen,[4] horribly plagued by a demon, whose own mother brought him [to Hypatius]. For he was unable to remain in one place, roving about to the point of absurdity. 9. He was so strong that he could overpower ten men and break the chains around his hands as if they were made of wood. 10. After staying at the monastery and regaining

---

[1] What this means is unclear; perhaps the woman is accusing herself or beating her body in a masochistic way.

[2] Mark 1:24.

[3] This person is otherwise unknown.

[4] This person is otherwise unknown.

his health through the slave of God's prayers, he returned again to his youthful and worldly disorder and wandered about.[5] 11. Consequently, again the demon attacked him, and again they bound him and brought him to the saint. God cured him through the saint's petition. 12. But he did this one time, a second time, a third time, and a fourth time over the course of a four-year period. 13. During the most recent one, the demon attempted to make him commit murder. While the brothers were taking a midday nap, he lifted a large bench and intended to rain blows down upon their heads. The Lord, however, did not allow him to do it, for "the Lord protects the lives[6] of his devotees."[7] 14. One of the young [brothers] woke up and got control of him; there was a struggle, but thirty-six [brothers] managed, with difficulty, to tie him up. 15. He bit two of them—one on the arm, and as for the other, he bit off his finger. 16. The Lord, though, through the prayers of his slave Hypatius cured him in the end, and the demon no longer came near him, and he healed those who were bitten.

17. They brought another peasant by the name of Tryphon,[8] whose foot had decayed, to be healed by the saint. 18. But the slave of God summoned an experienced physician so that he might skillfully make a cut at the bone called the fibula, but when he said, "We should instead amputate his foot from the knee down," Hypatius prayed and ordered the bone to be fixed. 19. And so, taking his gimlet[9] and mallet, the physician cut the bone and it cracked loudly. While the peasant was reeling in pain, he said, "What are you doing to me?" 20. The physician courteously said to him, "We are separating your foot from the bone." 21. And after they removed the bone from the astragalus, a little while passed and the Lord cured him—he had a foot without a bone. 22. He

---

[5] See 2 Thess 3:11.

[6] Or "souls."

[7] Ps 96(97):10.

[8] This person is otherwise unknown.

[9] A surgical tool used to bore into flesh and bone.

ran about like everyone else and worked more than anyone else, and he had no impediment, so that all the onlookers glorified God.

23. Again, at another time, the brothers were digging a well two fathoms deep when they brought up a huge stone, so big that it took eight men to lift it. Those at the top put it to the side, but the stone fell back down and knocked two brothers down into the well. 24. Saint Hypatius was there, saw what happened, and cried out right when they were falling, saying, "Blessed be the Lord!" 25. And neither one of them was struck by the stone at all; one just got his clothes wet. 26. For there was water in the well, which is why they were digging and found the stone. They were looking for water so that they might irrigate their garden.

27. There was another man, who served as a secretary in the prefect's office, by the name of Egersius;[10] he was a middle-aged Hellene.[11] 28. Wanting to save him, God arranged for him to lose his documents. He also heard about Hypatius and went to him, falling before him and saying, 29. "Pray that my documents be found, and I will believe in God. If they are not found, I'll put myself to flight or come up with another idea to keep the ruler from terminating me."[12] 30. But [Hypatius] instructed him with an exhortation and, praying to God, said to him, 31. "Go! A person will meet you who says that your documents have been found, and immediately do what you promised God you would do— become a Christian!" 32. And so, when he went back three miles, when he was just about to ferry across [the Bosporus to Constantinople], he heard that the documents had been found. 33. For his slave chased after him, thinking that he had run away. When he met up with him, he announced to him that the documents had been found. 34. Overjoyed, [Egersius] returned to Hypatius and gave thanks to the Lord; not only did he believe in God and get baptized, but he also made his renunciation. 35. After posting his

---

[10] This person is otherwise unknown.
[11] A non-Christian.
[12] Perhaps "executing me."

slave back at the archival repository, he led an august and reverent life. 36. He became a receptionist [at the monastic hostel], and on a daily basis he received both monks and those who were sufficiently poor, doling out the nourishment that God gave him while he was in the [government's] service.

Chapter 41

1. Again, at another time, an archimandrite by the name of Alexander, who came from the west, dwelled in the city together with roughly one hundred brothers.[1] 2. His regimen was glorious to everyone, for he was a zealot in the extreme, and, motivated by zeal, he rebuked rulers whenever he became aware of something inappropriate. 3. For their part, they acted with common cause and exiled him, so that he went back into his homeland. 4. After he left the city, together with the brothers he came and sought refuge in [the church of the Holy] Apostle[s] near Hypatius's monastery. 5. And the bishop sent hordes to chase them away from there at the bidding of the rulers. But when the hordes came and bludgeoned the brothers along with Alexander, they were ejected from the church of the Holy Apostles; they [even] wounded some of the brothers. 6. In the end, as the brothers were carrying their

[1] As this section makes clear, this monk is Alexander, the leader of the "Sleepless Monks." He is the subject of his own *Life*. Originally from the Greek islands (thus, west of Constantinople), he traveled to Syria and Mesopotamia where he developed a monastic regimen that included continual prayer (practiced by monks taking turns performing a continuous liturgy of hymns and prayers), an assertion of his own charismatic authority over that of the church and government, voluntary poverty, and a refusal to work. He inspired a heated response when he brought his monks to Constantinople in the 420s and began to rouse the city's poor against ecclesiastical and governmental elites (as he had done previously in Antioch). A later critique by Nilus of Ancyra also condemns him on economic grounds, accusing him of pulling young men out of local work forces. His presence and activity in the imperial capital probably spurred a synod of church leaders in 426 to indict his activity under the broader condemnation of wandering ascetics known as Messalians. For Hypatius's positive attitude toward Alexander, see the introduction to this volume.

Abba (he was unable to walk because of the blows), they passed by the monastery. 7. And so, as they were going, Hypatius went out there and stopped them. He then led them into the monastery, offered them refreshment, and tended to their wounds. 8. The bishop of Chalcedon[2] sent word to Hypatius, saying, "Because you welcomed Alexander, you must be chased out tomorrow along with him." 9. But he said to the messenger, "Tell the bishop, 'He who touches him will be as one who touches the apple of his eye.'"[3] 10. And so the bishop sent martyrial decans,[4] poor people, artisans, clergy members, and two mules so that, once they had situated [Alexander and Hypatius] on them, they might lead them into exile. 11. Some peasants were distressed by those who sent for Hypatius and said, "Order it and, once we've gathered together, we'll chase them away." 12. But he responded to them, "Let it be, children. If our being persecuted isn't something that comes from God, then my God will persecute them!" 13. When all the brothers were ready, and each was even willing to take on the road a book [as] a blessing, behold! A decan on horseback from the imperial court, who had learned what had happened, came upon the horde and said, 14. "Get me a shorthand writer and some papyrus! Give me your names! The empress[5] sent me to find out who is persecuting the slaves of God!" 15. And as soon as they heard him, they covered their faces [in shame] and ran away, so that none of them remained behind. 16. And the Scripture was fulfilled that said, "How will one chase away a thousand, and two remove ten thousand, if God did not allow them to do so?"[6] 17. "For the Lord's angel will set itself around those who fear him and will rescue them."[7] 18. Well then, for several days after that, a decent number

---

[2] Presumably Eulalius; see 32.12–20, 33.4.

[3] Zech 2:12 (LXX).

[4] Workers at the martyrium.

[5] Presumably Aelia Eudocia, the wife of Theodosius II.

[6] Deut 32:30.

[7] Ps 33:8 (34:7).

of soldiers guarded the monastery. So after Hypatius spent some time refreshing the flock, along with their shepherd, he sent [Alexander and his disciples] away. 19. They gave thanks and departed to make the greatest monastery in their own spot, fifteen miles away, where three hundred ascetics would live together, glorifying God incessantly. 20. These are the monks who live at the monastery of the Sleepless Ones.

Chapter 42

1. Someone else by the name of Macarius[1] became a disciple of Saint Hypatius. While he was living in the world, he possessed zeal but not much in the way of knowledge.[2] He had also lived with magicians, because of which he developed a secret abnormality in his mind—it was so secret that even he did not know it. 2. After he took the holy baptism, he was moved by zeal and yearning and went into the monastery, renounced the world, and became a monk. 3. So intensely did he drive headlong into persistent discipline—for he was quite well put together with respect to his body— that he performed the work of three people, or if ever they needed to till a garden, dig a trench for the vineyard, or do some other hard work, what was required for the job would be assigned to him while the others would work with [animal] hair. 5. One of them was a copyist, one a clothes washer and seamster, one a porter (for while there was one door, no one could just come and go), one tended the sick, and one waited around to receive guests. 6. During the week, all the workers traded jobs with each other, but in addition to the common liturgy for all of them, each one, amidst his work, recited a psalm and gave a prayer to God. 7. One could not just switch from the task to which he was assigned to another but remained in the station where he was bid.

8. Macarius, though, to whatever commission he was charged, eagerly and seriously dedicated himself to the toil because he was truly enslaved to God in accordance with the verse "far greater in

[1] This person is otherwise unknown.
[2] Rom 10:2.

labors."[3] 9. Indeed, exercising tremendous self-control, he kept vigil, and often he prayed Terce[4] after having stood upright throughout the night. 10. In addition to the common psalmody and vigil of all, he would recite all of David's [psalms] twice in a twenty-four-hour period. 11. He possessed such love for the brothers that he never sought his own respite, but only that of his brother. 12. Enslaved to God like this, he also received from God the cure for his former madness. 13. And so [Macarius had spent] eighteen years in the monastery without [the Devil] being able to get the upper hand on him in any respect. [But] the Devil found a crack in his humility and brought up in [Macarius's] thought his toils for virtue by introducing certain impressions to him in the form of Christ. Finally he took him captive with self-conceit, thrusting this into his thoughts: 14. "You are righteous beyond everyone else, for you are more disciplined than everyone else, and Jesus loves you, dwells in you, and speaks to the brothers through you." 15. As time went by, Hypatius and some of the brothers could tell from his words that [Macarius] had gone astray, and [Hypatius] offered him instruction. 16. And [Macarius] was unpersuaded but mocked all of them, for he had been ravaged by a contrary callousness, something that had happened to him because of his lack of discernment. 17. So crackbrained was he that he shouted at Saint Hypatius audaciously, 18. "Usurper of Christ! The right hand of God[5] is upon my head, and Jesus converses with me and is revealed by me, and Jesus said to me, 'I am granting you a thousand bishops so that you may rule them as archbishop!'" 19. But Hypatius felt compassion for him, wanting to avoid having the deceived [Macarius] leave the monastery. [Hypatius] cast iron [chains] around his feet so that, closely guarded, he might come to himself. 20. And after a few days, Macarius said to Hypatius, "Release me and give me one brother so that I may leave and gather

---

[3] 2 Cor 11:23.
[4] The third-hour (9 a.m.) prayer.
[5] See Ps 117(118):15-16.

the thousands that Jesus promised to me." 21. Hypatius responded to him, "I would like you not to leave. But should you refuse, I won't be giving you another brother. If you want to go, you go alone!" 22. And so, after he left, he approached the holy mysteries[6] without having gotten a blessing or making peace with his spiritual father. 23. This was the pattern and sequence that prevailed: one who left the monastery—even if he joined a community somewhere else, even if he was about to go on a journey—first he had to go and make peace with the priest and father and get a blessing, and, finally, he could thus approach the holy mysteries unhindered and spotless, in accordance with the commandment of Christ that says, 24. "If you offer your gift, first be reconciled to your brother."[7] One time, someone out of thoughtlessness had fellowship without getting a blessing, and he was punished by God with a terrible punishment until he went to Hypatius, prayed with him, and was cured. 25. But the wretched Macarius, who fully needed the tears of the slaves of God, spent four years [in punishment]; he neither went to his father and made peace nor gathered a single one of the thousand. 26. Not making peace with his father became for him something worse than any physical harm. 27. One year after Hypatius's death, some brothers brought him, now punished with an illness, to the monastery; Hypatius's disciples were moved by pity and received him right at the point when his flesh and bones had begun to waste away. 28. For eighty days, he took no nourishment but cried out and said, 29. "To think I rejected Saint Hypatius, my father!" 30. Now sober in his mind, he cried out, saying, "Behold my disease! They are horribly flagellating me with whips!"

31. Upon saying these words, he gave up the ghost. And they buried him with the [other deceased] brothers in the place where the brothers [who were alive] finished their prayers each day. 32. For since he undertook [his lifestyle] with a lack of discernment and a dismissiveness as someone inexperienced in temperance,

---

[6] That is, Macarius went straight to receive the Eucharist.
[7] Matt 5:24.

he did not remain standing in his battles [against demons]; for this reason, the Lord had compassion on him and did not deprive him of brotherly fellowship,[8] a mercy that, by means of the intercessions of all the saints and our father Hypatius, we, along with all the slaves of God, hope to find with the Lord on that day—Amen. 33. We have mentioned him [here] for a demonstration of the profit that exists in humility. For if someone were to possess myriad virtues without humility, he would labor in vain. 34. Everyone who is arrogant is an abomination in the sight of the Lord,[9] and he builds a house on sand,[10] "and there is contempt for the proud."[11] 35. But the Lord looks upon the prayer of the humble:[12] "I have been humbled and he saved me."[13] 36. For notice how the brother Macarius practiced discipline so that, regarding himself, he might be thought to be something. 37. If God's mercy had not outrun him, he would have destroyed everything. 38. And so good deeds are such that if anyone does one, he should truthfully say in his heart, 39. "I am not worthy of being called a slave of the Lord,[14] nor in the slightest am I sufficient [to be called] a slave of God. For God, who gives grace, performs the good deeds and deems us worthy of knowing how to perform a good deed; he is 'the one who teaches humanity knowledge.'"[15] 40. For he said, "Avoid wickedness and do good."[16] "The Lord will reward whatever good someone does."[17]

[8] That is, he was buried with his monastic brothers.

[9] See Prov 16:5.

[10] See Matt 7:26.

[11] See Ps 122(123):4.

[12] Ps 101:18 (102:17).

[13] Ps 114:6 (LXX).

[14] See Luke 15:19.

[15] See Ps 93(94):10.

[16] Ps 33:15 (34:16).

[17] See Eph 6:8.

Chapter 43

1. At another time, while standing during the service, [Hypatius] smelled a pungent stench. Indeed, many people used to come from the city to listen to him, and they benefited from his holy prayers. 2. But at the end of the service, as if by a divine power, he called out the person from whom the stench emanated and, publicly addressing him, said, 3. "Where are you from? What's your business here, and what are you carrying?" He responded, "I am from Antioch, and I want to become a Christian." 4. After examining him, [Hypatius] found a rag [wrapped around] him like a belt, three fingers wide, and he inquired of him, "What could this be?[1] 5. For during the prayer, I smelled a Satanic stench." It was with difficulty that [the man] confessed that the garment itself was from Artemis; immediately [Hypatius] ordered it be burned. 6. Well, even though the garment was cast into the fire, it did not burn but rather became a spherical object. 7. At that point, once the saint had performed a prayer with other brothers, he crushed it into dust by stomping it with his feet. He mixed [the dust] with soil, threw it into the latrine, and said to the man, 8. "If you want to become a Christian, bring me your [magical] book and all your magical paraphernalia." And he dispatched a brother with him, but [the man] drew back and escaped.

9. At another time, he heard that someone was practicing divination. He summoned him, saying, "Come so that I might honor you with dignity." So when he came, he said, 10. "I hear that you tell the future, and, if someone loses something, you tell him who stole it. And I exhort you, tell me how you do this so that I might

---

[1] Acts 2:12.

learn how I can honor you with respect." 11. [The man] began speaking excitedly, "If someone tells me about some issue, immediately, in the night, it is revealed to me, and I tell them, so that each of them goes away and sacrifices either a cow, sheep, or bird at the idol-temple. Thus it's left for me to say what an angel reveals." 12. Hypatius made it so that these words were written down, and once he had locked [the man] up, he said to him, 13. "So, it's through you, therefore, that Satan teaches human beings to worship idols? Believe you me! You are not to leave here, lest Satan uses you to destroy souls. Even though I've locked you in a cell, I'm providing you with bread for the rest of your life." 14. For he was an old man. While he spent a little time there, it was with difficulty that the priests in the neighboring region gave Hypatius their word that they would not let him practice these things [ever again]. 15. And he took a written oath from him and thus let him go. He died soon thereafter.

16. At another time, again he heard that there was a house three mile markers away where some forty men dwelled and sacrificed to idols. 17. And one of them, by the name of Helpidius,[2] wanted to become a Christian; he did not conduct the lawless practices with them. Therefore, after repeatedly flogging him, they threw him out, saying, "Let's see how Christ helps you [now]!" 18. Laid low by the blows, he developed terrible sores. When Hypatius learned about these matters, he immediately sent an ass and brought him to the monastery; he offered relief, as if he were [Helpidius's] father, and treated the sores. 19. By Hypatius's hands, he regained his health and then was deemed worthy of baptism. He made his renunciation and was devotedly enslaved to the Lord for thirty years, and, when he blessedly came to the end of his life, he found respite at a noble old age. 20. Hypatius, though, sent word to those forty men, saying, "Repent and become Christians! If you don't, God's wrath will quickly overtake you!" 21. They refused to

---

[2] This person is otherwise unknown.

obey, and before one year had passed, God's wrath overtook them. 22. Some of them came to their demise by a demon of bitter death and others disintegrated; the house became vacant, as if no one had ever lived there, as it is written: "Let their courtyard become deserted, and in their dwellings let no one dwell."[3]

[3] Ps 68:26 (69:25).

Chapter 44

1. At yet another time, a certain chamberlain by the name of Euphemia[1] was tormented by a terrible demon, and she sent for the saint, begging him to come and offer a prayer because she was in danger. 2. So after she begged him many times, he relented because she was completely Christian. And once he left, he made his prayer and right afterward partook of nourishment. 3. And when he went to the monastery, he prayed for her and petitioned Christ. 4. Then the demons causing her difficulties appeared to Hypatius, saying, 5. "Why are you forcing us to leave her? If you chase us from here, we'll come and afflict you!" 6. Nevertheless, he did it. Indeed, while she regained her health, they afflicted the saint so terribly that he was ill for twenty days. 7. In the end, he became healthy, and the Lord rendered them ineffective.

8. Another person, a count by the name of Helpidius,[2] the emperor's master builder, was tormented terribly by a demon in his body, and, consumed as he was by terrible pains, he screamed out. 9. Once he had heard about the saint, he went to him with the help of a bed and some slaves. 10. At the same time, Saint Hypatius performed a prayer on his behalf, and while the man sat on his bed, [Hypatius] placed his hand where he was hurting, and it grew more tolerable for him. 11. But the man wouldn't let [Hypatius] leave, for just as he was getting up to leave, immediately the pains tormented him, and he let out a great scream. 12. As if boasting, he said, "My wealth can't be boiled down to a particular number!"

---

[1] This person is otherwise unknown.

[2] This person is otherwise unknown, and he is a different person than the Helpidius mentioned at 43.17.

13. While he spent a few days there, the day laborers and impoverished workers went and approached the saint, saying, "Helpidius has treated us unjustly," and, "He's gotten his wealth from exploiting us." 14. Having come to know this, the saint said to Helpidius, "It's been revealed to me that you will die. God has punished you because you've treated many people unjustly. 15. So go and get your house in order, and if you've committed any injustice, make amends so that your soul may get some refreshment." 16. Having received this judgment, he departed deeply aggrieved. 17. But while he was intending to get his affairs in order, the physicians told him, at the suggestion of those who wanted to steal his wealth, "You're not going to die." 18. And within three days, he was struggling and cried out, "Where are you, Abba Hypatius?" 19. As he said these words, he gave up the ghost, but everyone glorified God because, if the saint uttered something, it immediately came to pass.

20. Another person, by the name of Antiochus,[3] beloved by the noble ranks, was under investigation for murder; so greatly was he oppressed by the demon that all who saw him were sympathetic. 21. They even brought him to several martyria for the reason of getting healed; then they led him to Hypatius, and the demon was so terrifying that for fifty days they could not fall asleep, not even for a single hour, because of his screaming. 22. But the Lord remained there at his side for one year and healed him, and finally he gave thanks to God, prostrating himself before and begging Hypatius to pray on his behalf. 23. He came from another cult,[4] but once he joined the orthodox faith, he made his renunciation and became so zealous for virtue, with God providing him discipline, that he truly became a disciple of Hypatius; that is to say, God perfected him in the saints' prayers, so that the Scripture was fulfilled that said, "That's the change that comes from the right hand of the highest."[5]

---

[3] This person is otherwise unknown.
[4] That is, a heretical Christian community.
[5] Ps 76:11 (77:10).

24. Another person, by the name of Dionysius,[6] was abused by a demon so much that his body, incited by his heart, jumped around everywhere, as if a seizure were happening. 25. Within a few days of going out to the slave of God, the Lord healed him. 26. Immediately he too renounced the world and became a slave of God and an authentic disciple of the saint.

27. Another person, a stonemason by trade, was enamored with the saint's regimen and yearned for it; he gave his word to the Abba that he would make a renunciation. 28. But after he left and some time had passed, he changed his mind. And God exacted punishment on his eyes, and he was terribly blinded. 29. As if explaining it to himself, he went and said, "By renouncing and denying God, I have sinned! And so now, pray that I may be healed! I will not reject him [again]!" 30. With Hypatius's prayer, the Lord healed him. And again, he left and denied his promise. 31. After a few days, he fell into a stone quarry and died, so that not even his bones would be seen, as it is written, 32. "It is a trap for a man to rashly consecrate his own things"[7] and after making the consecration to not hand them over. God does not compel us to make a renunciation. 33. Indeed, he grows irritated against us if we reject following through on our word after the agreement. For he says, "Pray and hand it over to the Lord our God."[8]

34. Another person, by the name of Polychronius,[9] had a terrible sore on his right foot, which made a gash [through] flesh and bone; it was impossible to determine the start or end of the sore, or how to treat it. 35. So as it worsened, he begged Saint Hypatius for treatment, promising to make his renunciation. 36. But the Abba said to him, "Let's pray to God that you get well, and in this—if he heals you—we may know that God summons you to be enslaved to him."

---

[6] This person is otherwise unknown.

[7] Prov 20:25.

[8] Ps 75:12 (76:11).

[9] This person is otherwise unknown.

37. And simply put, [Hypatius] was like a physician given by God to this region, and, in the style of Job, he was a foot to the lame, an eye to the blind, a staff to the disabled,[10] and a consolation to those who needed it, in accordance with the verse, 38. "From your soul give the hungry your bread,[11] and bring into your house the homeless poor and your light will rise early."[12]

39. But when you hear of a blind person, do not suppose that it is because he was blind from birth.[13] For [healing] this [kind of blindness] is possible for the Lord alone. 40. The same is true with lunatics, because no one can heal them except the Lord alone, who directs his kindness toward all people through the prayers of the saints, just as the Gospel tells us 41. that [the boy] was brought to his disciples and was not healed, but the Lord healed him.[14]

[10] Job 29:15-16.
[11] Isa 58:10.
[12] Isa 58:7-8.
[13] See John 9:1.
[14] See Matt 17:16-18.

Chapter 45

1. One time, he went to make an inspection of the brothers in the region of inner Bithynia, where the Rhebas River also is. 2. It was during that time when the detestable Artemis's processional basket, as they say, would appear.[1] Every year, people in the region guarded over the basket and for fifty days would not go out on any long journey. 3. When [Hypatius] wanted to pass through, the locals said to him, "Where are you going, man? The demon could meet you on the road. Don't pass through, for many people have been abused." 4. When Hypatius heard these words, he smiled and said, "You might be scared of these things, but I have Christ as my traveling companion." 5. So he was confident in his travel, "for the righteous is as bold as a lion."[2] 6. And a woman[3] as tall as ten men came from a distance to meet him. Whirling about, she was walking and feeding the pigs. 7. As soon as he saw her, he sealed himself and stood praying to God. 8. Immediately she became invisible, and the pigs fled with a great whoosh.

---

[1] The basket (*kálathos*), signifying fertility, was associated with local veneration of Artemis; it was held atop the head of a processional participant.

[2] Prov 28:1.

[3] The goddess Artemis.

Chapter 46

1. Another time, in autumn, he passed by Mount Olympus[1] with several brothers and suddenly stopped. 2. A gust of air and a gloomy cloud overshadowed them on the mountain, and those with him said to him, "Lord, pray that hail doesn't fall upon us!" 3. But Hypatius immediately spread out his arms in that spot and prayed to God. 4. Despite the ferocious storm that came, there was hardly any hail as they traveled two or three mile markers, nor did their sandals get wet at all. 5. When they got to the monastery to which they were going, the brothers there were surprised that there was no water at all on their clothes.

[1] The modern Uludağ.

Chapter 47

1. And so let no one fail to believe that it was God who performed these miracles through his slave. For in anticipation of this, the Lord said, 2. "Amen, I am telling you that if you have faith the size of a mustard seed, and you also tell this mountain, 'Get up and throw yourself into the sea,' it will be done,"[1] and, "Whatever you ask of my father in my name, he will give to you."[2] 3. "For all things are possible for the one who believes,"[3] and, "Everything that you ask of my father in prayer, as long as you believe, you will receive."[4] 4. In anticipation of this, the holy apostle explained unwavering faith by saying, 5. "Faith is the basis of things hoped for, a conviction in things not seen."[5]

6. Look, we say in Christ before God that in no way have we satisfactorily covered [all the deeds of] Hypatius, the slave of God, but in making our record, we have related the more important events for those who yearn to be enslaved to God. 7. And yet, again, we are not saying that it was Hypatius who ordered someone to be cured or bossed the demons around, but rather that he invoked Christ and was pleasing in his sight.[6] For everything that a righteous person does brings prosperity.[7] 8. He is favorable with the Lord on account of his loving him and with a fiery yearning

---

[1] Matt 17:20 and 21:21 combined.
[2] See John 15:16.
[3] Mark 9:23.
[4] See Matt 21:22.
[5] Heb 11:1.
[6] Heb 13:21.
[7] See Ps 1:3.

enacts [the Lord's] commands. That's why Christ equipped him with these [abilities]. 9. "Indeed, all things work to a good end for those who love Christ."[8]

[8] Rom 8:28.

Chapter 48

1. Additionally, he always taught as a father, saying,

Children, being Christian is not an accident. You must work hard, fight the good fight,[1] let yourself become worn down a little so that you can find much rest. 2. Take hold of eternal life;[2] run toward the prize of your upward calling.[3] 3. Learn to do good;[4] be courageous in the Lord, and be strong powerfully,[5] because the contest is not against blood and flesh, but against the wicked demons[6] and the passions of the flesh. 4. Therefore take up the whole armor of God, gird your loins in truth, strap your feet in preparation for the Gospel of peace, and take up the shield of faith, the helmet of salvation, and the sword of the Spirit, which is God's word, by means of all prayer and supplication.[7] 5. And so, having armed ourselves with these weapons on account of ineffable reward for righteousness, let us be dedicated as pleasing soldiers of Christ,[8] let us wage war against the Devil's wiles[9] and fight back against sin to the point of blood.[10] 6. For it belongs to the mature to have sense faculties that have been trained in discernment of

[1] 1 Tim 6:12.
[2] 1 Tim 6:12.
[3] Phil 3:14.
[4] Isa 1:17.
[5] Eph 6:10.
[6] See Eph 6:12.
[7] See Eph 6:13-18.
[8] See 2 Tim 2:3.
[9] Eph 6:11.
[10] Heb 12:4.

good and evil[11] in accordance with the verse, 7. "far greater in labors,"[12] in vigils, in fasts, "in cold and nakedness,"[13] "in beatings, in prisons, in riots."[14] 8. If anyone treats Christ philosophically in outward appearance or [mere] words, take no heed of that person. For the kingdom of heaven depends not on word but on power,[15] and not [as a wolf] in the outward appearance of sheep,[16] but rather as the Lord said, "You will know them by their fruits."[17] 9. If anyone is found performing the commands of Christ with yearning, and his deeds correspond to his good words, and he always possesses a broken heart,[18] he will despise himself night and day. 10. And the one who does such things stands in truth. Cleave to such a person, and let us accept him as a father, a teacher, a brother, a member of our own faith,[19] a faithful friend, and someone who genuinely shares the same soul as us, in accordance with the verse, 11. "Stand in the midst of elders—who is wise? Attach yourself to him,"[20] and, "If you know an intelligent person, rise early for him."[21] 12. For he who is joined to saints will be made holy. 13. And again, "Do not dwell with an angry man; never learn his ways, and never ensnare your soul."[22] 14. For bad company corrupts good habits.[23] 15. If you must be joined [to anyone], be joined to a good and wise person. For the good person

---

[11] Heb 5:14.
[12] 2 Cor 11:23.
[13] 2 Cor 11:27.
[14] 2 Cor 6:5.
[15] 1 Cor 4:20.
[16] See Matt 7:15.
[17] Matt 7:16.
[18] See Ps 50:19 (51:17).
[19] See Rom 12:5.
[20] Sir 6:34.
[21] Sir 6:36.
[22] See Prov 22:24-25.
[23] 1 Cor 15:33.

produces good out of the good treasure in his heart,[24] and he always offers good counsel for you. 16. He wants to make you his equal and guide you to God in accordance with the [scriptural] phrase, "I want all to be as I am. 17. But each has his own gift from God."[25]

18. Indeed Hypatius himself held his disciples to so high a standard that they would need to serve and be slaves to God, as he was. 19. He trained his children in a mature heart. And they revered him exuberantly: with fear they obeyed him, and with modesty they honored him as their spiritual father. 20. He always taught them by saying,

Children, let us not succumb to acedia[26] in this brief age, for the work of virtue is slight and the promises are great. 21. Through brief toils, let us focus on entering the kingdom of heaven and being enlisted as citizens for the portion of the saints' inheritance.[27] 22. For the sufferings of the present time are not comparable to the glory that will soon be revealed in us.[28] 23. While we still have an opportunity,[29] let us pay attention to ourselves and remain patient as we become pleasing to the Lord, so that we will not have any regret or tears when there is no opportunity for repentance or doing a good deed. 24. For the easiness of this world and its anxieties distract our mind so that, even if we come to our senses, we cannot clearly devote our attention to God and make ourselves safe from every evil. 25. He who has lived in carelessness and satiated his stomach cannot be illuminated with the illumination of the inner person in the secret workshop of his heart. 26. For

---

[24] Luke 6:45.
[25] 1 Cor 7:7.
[26] See 24.91, with the note.
[27] Col 1:12.
[28] Rom 8:18.
[29] Gal 6:10.

the one who realizes that the mental war must be fought mightily presses on into security and pays attention to himself; fleeing all earthly things, he will weld his mind with God by, in his yearning, fastening it to a vigilant soul, night and day. 27. By the grace of God, he will begin to illuminate the inner person and walk down the path of salvation. 28. And so he must suffer many afflictions in his trials thus to attain this step. 29. But if trials and tribulations [still] attack him after he has received grace, he should endure in the good, petitioning God at all times. 30. And do not succumb to acedia by losing heart amidst tribulation, but put up with it nobly and endure. 31. For love endures all things;[30] the grace of God will immediately turn back again and encamp within him. 32. Look, children, for your benefit, I am compelled to say aloud what should remain concealed, lest I incur some damage by boasting. However, Christ the Master knows that I am speaking for God's glory and your benefit. 33. For I have already spent sixty years in the monastic life; I have been satiated with neither sleep nor bread nor water, so that I could be an authentic and faithful slave, so that I might be deemed worthy of hearing from my Lord, 34. "Well done, good and faithful slave! In a few things, you have been trustworthy; I will put you in charge of many things. Enter into the joy of your Lord."[31] 35. I do not reckon myself the pinnacle [of monastic success] in comparison to the least of the slaves of God. Indeed, since the time when I fell into my anxieties for the brothers and began to feel responsible for setting each one right, the purity of my mind, which I held out toward God, has wholly become a wasteland. 36. For back then, I used to be free from anxiety, and I eagerly paid attention to God and myself, and [consequently] I possessed a bit of license[32] [with God].

---

[30] 1 Cor 13:7.

[31] Matt 25:21.

[32] In Greek, *parrhēsía*. The level of holiness that Hypatius had achieved allowed him to speak freely and openly with God.

37. Well, since he was speaking these words in slight distress, one of the brothers responded to him and said, 38. "Lord Abba, back then you saved just yourself through God, but now [you have saved] many people. And the damage you incurred there you have restored twofold here. For the Lord Jesus came to save all people." When he heard this, [Hypatius] rejoiced in the Lord.

39. At another time, when many people were crowding around him and pulling him to many distractions—to illnesses or to issuing responses to the cellarer or to the porter about guests, to affairs concerning the poor or concerning the brothers—40. while they were crowding around him, a certain brother who was present said to him, "Lord, aren't all these distractions still pulling your mind away from God now?" 41. He answered by saying, "I trust in the grace of God. Even if there were even more [distractions], my mind would remain vigilant toward God."

Chapter 49

1. And so, when he had grown old and his gray hair had become like snow on his entire head and beard—for his mien was also aged and favorable, as one truly belonging to a priest of God and a father—he enthusiastically tended a small vineyard so that his ailments would have consolation. 2. Another ascetic by the name of Zeno[1] came to him and, while [Hypatius] was on his way to the vineyard, met with him on the road and said to him, "Are you Lord Hypatius?" [Hypatius] said to him, "Yes." 3. And [Zeno] said to him, "I sent [a letter] to you so that my bones would find repose near you." 4. [Zeno's] appearance was that of the most insignificant person. Indeed, because he humbled himself, his dress was so meager that he looked like a peasant. 5. [Hypatius] received him, and [Zeno] spent roughly ten days there, working extremely hard. And when [Zeno] saw a brother being carried to his grave, he stood there and said, 6. "My God, let me—a humble man—find repose here too." And on that very day, he became ill; eight days later, he found repose. 7. There was found in his bag a letter of recommendation, because he was a priest, though he was not at all acknowledged [as such] by anyone.[2]

---

[1] This person is otherwise unknown; he is almost certainly a different person than the Zeno of 28.38–57.

[2] That is, when Zeno arrived, he had concealed his clerical identity, which was only revealed by a letter of recommendation that he possessed in his bag.

Chapter 50

1. And three months later, when Saint Hypatius was eighty years old and had nobly shepherded Christ's flock for forty years and devotedly administered the priesthood, he was proclaimed a perfect and pleasing slave of Christ, having sent forth eighty of his disciples to God before himself.[1]

2. During those three months, he said, "Children, a terrible wrath hangs over the world, and it is good to return to the Lord before the trial comes about. 3. Well, pay close attention to yourselves, for I have fulfilled my role. 4. And focus on being authentically enslaved to the Lord; in fear and trembling, work for your own salvation[2] in the same way that you have watched me do. 5. And as I handed down to you, hold fast the traditions that God taught me. 6. Indeed, I have trust in God that, if you perform his work, God will not forsake you. Just as he has shown me mercy, so too has he shown you mercy; you will receive a full reward for patience, and I will welcome you truly as my very own children, so that we of the same feeling are deemed worthy to dwell together with the saints."

[1] That is, eighty of his disciples had died before Hypatius over the course of his forty-year career as the abbot of the Rufinianae.

[2] See Phil 2:12.

Chapter 51

1. As he was speaking these words, all of us were strengthened and wept, knowing that he was praying for death. After having spent five days in illness, on the sixth day, which was a Sunday, he said, "Summon the brothers so that I may give them communion."[1] 2. He had already begun to lose consciousness while another man held his hand in the midst of his giving the blessing, and he whispered an antiphonal psalm, "Come, let us rejoice in the Lord."[2] 3. But as they were singing psalms and taking communion out of his hand, the brothers wept, because they all knew that it was actually the angels, who would receive him, who were rejoicing. That's why they were singing the psalm, "Come, let us rejoice in the Lord."

4. He believed that he saw some bishops and some of his close friends coming to get him; as he was beginning to lose consciousness and as he was receiving blessings from someone standing nearby, he believed that the person present was the one bestowing [blessings] on some people there, and no one appeared to receive them and the one who was present welcomed them again.[3] 5. But all the friends, monks, and clergy members who came received a blessing from him. 6. Once he blessed all of them and gave them the kiss of peace, he found repose and was deposited with the holy fathers, leaving behind a congregation of as many as fifty brothers, whom he handed down to one particular successor of his to lead them.[4]

---

[1] The eucharistic elements.

[2] Ps 94(95):1.

[3] The meaning of this sentence is unclear.

[4] This is presumably Callinicus, the author of the hagiography.

7. A great number of bishops came, along with everyone who loved him on account of his excellent lifestyle, so that a crowd formed from this great Christ-loving people and from the entire monastery; when everyone had kindled their candles, they tended to his corpse with devotion amidst psalms and hymns. 8. Well, all the bearers of his precious body wept as if they had become orphans of a great father. 9. They then peacefully deposited his holy remains in a stone sarcophagus within his monastery's hallowed chapel, the building in which the brothers sent up their prayers. 10. As he was being deposited, though, the crowds tore the funeral dressing into pieces, wanting to get from his garments the grace of his blessing; one person cut the canvas with a sword, while another made a cut from his garment, and another cut hair from his beard. 11. Then, the slave of God, Urbicius,[5] made an offering [over] his sarcophagus. 12. Laid next to him was Saint Ammonius,[6] the great ascetic of the desert, about whom it was said that he cut off his ear because he did not want to accept priestly ordination,[7] whose regimen was exceptional and admired by all those who love the Lord.

13. Well, that's how we too should practice asceticism, brothers. For the Lord also glorifies those who glorify him and not only registers his genuine slaves in the kingdom,[8] but also honorably holds up their regimen to everyone as a model for good imitation.

[5] See 12.4. This is the same person who financed the renovations and expansion of the Rufinianae.

[6] One of the Egyptian Tall Brothers, who populated the monastery prior to Hypatius's arrival. His remains were housed in the chapel of the Rufinianae. For further discussion, see the introduction to this volume.

[7] The story of Ammonius's cutting off his ear to avoid ordination was well known in late antiquity; see Socrates, *Ecclesiastical History* 4.23.74.

[8] See Luke 10:20.

Chapter 52

1. And so thirty days had not passed when hail suddenly fell on those places so that the vineyard, fully ripe, was finally plucked by the hail. 2. Indeed, the hail was as large as stone, possessing on it something [that looked] like a man's eyeball, as if to mean, "Look out for what's coming!" 3. Within another five months, there were great earthquakes, which also lasted for a good stretch of time, and the barbarian race of the Huns grew so dominant in Thrace that more than a hundred cities were taken; Constantinople was placed in imminent danger, and most people fled from it. 4. It was so bad that even monks wanted to run away to Jerusalem, for [the Huns] came close to approaching and devastating Constantinople. 5. Murders and bloodshed were so widespread that the dead could not be laid out for counting. 6. They brought bloodshed to both churches and monasteries and killed most of the monks and virgins, so that even [the monastery of] Saint Alexander was devastated. They seized all the money and treasures in it, which had never happened before. 7. For although the Huns had frequently passed by before [the monastery of] Saint Alexander was fortified, none of them had ever dared to approach the martyrium. 8. They so desolated Thrace that it could never be revitalized and become as it had been, like it was before. 9. As for us, though, we were awestruck when we remembered that these were the events foretold by Saint Hypatius at the moment of his death.[1] How could he have known, except that the Lord disclosed it to him?

---

[1] See 50.2.

Chapter 53

1. But he also had one sister, who was married once but became a widow and had one daughter. She made a renunciation and was enslaved to Christ, and she found repose three days before her brother. 2. But her daughter was married once (and she had her own daughter) and, with her husband, made a renunciation. 3. Her husband, who became a deacon, found repose, but she ardently attached herself to God, enslaved to him night and day.[1] 4. And so Saint Hypatius did all things in line with our holy father Antony, even with respect to his sister.[2] 5. Just as [Antony] had one sister, so too did [Hypatius]. Yes, while he was going about in the flesh, Saint Hypatius used to say, 6. "Children, know that I regard our father Saint Antony as just after the holy apostles. He embraced me, he blessed me, and, after performing a prayer, he dismissed me."

---

[1] See Luke 2:37.

[2] The famous Egyptian monk, who was the subject of Athanasius of Alexandria's *Life of Antony*. For further discussion of the influence of the *Life of Antony* on the *Life of Hypatius*, see the introduction to this volume.

Chapter 54

1. After these things, someone came looking for the presbyter Zeno, and when we said, "He did not tell us that he was a priest," he immediately responded by saying, 2. "This Zeno, the man whom you considered to be insignificant, was a steward of eight hundred brothers, and he told me while he was alive (for my friend happened to be from Alexandria and the desert), 'I have received correspondence from the Lord: "Go to Hypatius and die there." 3. And so be convinced that immediately after I die and go to God, I will take Abba Hypatius right behind me.'" 4. Yes, Abba Hypatius survived for three months after Zeno and found repose in accordance with the oracle of God, which was disclosed to Zeno. 5. "And when I arrived here at the monastery while Zeno was still alive"— that elderly father said—"Zeno gave a sign to me and commanded me not to say anything to you about knowing him." 6. Zeno's monastery was located next to the Red Sea, through which the people of Israel passed. 7. Barbarians shed blood at that monastery. Those who lived there always held Zeno to be a prophet.

Chapter 55

1. And the aforementioned brother Polychronius,[1] the man with the pain in his foot, to whom Saint Hypatius said, 2. "If you are healed, become a monk if God provides [it for you]," he became a monk and a slave of God according to the prophecy of our father Hypatius.

[1] See 44.34.

Chapter 56

1. Holding together love and harmony with each other in Christ, his disciples were enslaved to God as they celebrated their father's memory. They held to his exhortations, and they tried to present themselves to God as respectable workers, since through the prayers of the saints and our sacred father Hypatius, God provided grace to them. 2. They followed in the father's footsteps in Christ, accomplishing the father's traditions and his spiritual way of life, and forming a spiritual chorus, they sent up hymns to God night and day, glorifying the Father, Son, and the Holy Spirit, to whom belongs all glory, honor, and adoration, now, always, forever and ever. Amen.

Bibliography

Primary Sources

Acts of the Blessed Monk, Abraham of Qidun. Ed. T. J. Lamy. "Acta Beati Abrahae Kidunaiae Monachi." *Analecta Bollandiana* 10 (1891): 5–49.

Acts of John. Ed. Eric Junod and Jean-Daniel Kaestli. *Acta Iohannis. Praefatio – Textus*. Corpus Christianorum, Series Apocryphorum 1. Turnhout: Brepols, 1983.

Athanasius. *Life of Antony*. Ed. and trans. G. J. M. Bartelink. *Athanase d'Alexandrie. Vie d'Antoine*. Sources chrétiennes 400. Paris: Éditions du Cerf, 1994.

Callinicus. *Life of Hypatius*. Ed. and trans. G. J. M. Bartelink. *Callinicos. Vie d'Hypatios*. Sources chrétiennes 177. Paris: Éditions du Cerf, 1971. *Acta Sanctorum Junii, Tomus III*: De S. Hypatii Abb. In Rufinianis. Antwerp, 1701.

Claudian. *Against Rufinus*. Trans. Neil W. Bernstein. *The Complete Works of Claudian*. London and New York: Routledge, 2023.

Cyril of Scythopolis. *Life of Saba*. Ed. Eduard Schwartz. *Kyrillos von Skythopolis*. Texte und Untersuchungen 49.2. Leipzig: Hinrichs, 1939.

Ephrem. *Hymns of Abraham of Qidun and Julian of Saba*. Ed. Edmund Beck. *Des heiligen Ephraem des Syrers Hymnen auf Abraham Kidunaya und Julianos Saba*. Corpus Scriptorum Christianorum Orientalium 322. Scriptores Syri 140. Leuven: Peeters, 1972.

Gregory of Nazianzus. *Oration 8: In Praise of His Sister Gorgonia*. Patrologia Graeca 35:789–817.

Gregory of Nyssa. *Life of Macrina*. Ed. and trans. Pierre Maraval. *Grégoire de Nysse. Vie de sainte Macrine*. Sources chrétiennes 178. Paris: Éditions du Cerf, 1971.

History of the Monks of Egypt. Ed. and trans. A.-J. Festugière. *Historia monachorum in Aegypto. Édition critique du texte grec.* Subsidia Hagiographica 34. Brussels: Société de Bollandistes, 1961.

Iamblichus. *On the Pythagorean Life.* Ed. Ulrich Klein and Ludwig Deubner. *Iamblichi. De vita Pythagorica liber.* Bibliotheca scriptorum Graecorum et Romanorum Teubneriana. Stuttgart: Teubner, 1975.

Jerome. *Life of Hilarion.* Ed. Edgardo Morales. *Jérôme. Trois vies de moines (Paul, Malchus, Hilarion).* Sources chrétiennes 508. Paris: Éditions du Cerf, 2007.

Jerome. *Life of Malchus.* Ed. Edgardo Morales. *Jérôme. Trois vies de moines (Paul, Malchus, Hilarion).* Sources chrétiennes 508. Paris: Éditions du Cerf, 2007.

Jerome. *Life of Paul.* Ed. Edgardo M. Morales. *Jérôme. Trois vies de moines (Paul, Malchus, Hilarion).* Sources chrétiennes 508. Paris: Éditions du Cerf, 2007.

Koriwn. *The Life of Mashtots' By His Disciple Koriwn.* Trans. Abraham Terian. Oxford Early Christian Texts. Oxford: Oxford University Press, 2022.

Life of Alexander the Sleepless. Ed. E. de Stroope. *La vie d'Alexandre d'Acémète.* Patrologia Orientalis 6. Paris: Firmin-Didot, 1911. Translated by Daniel Caner in *Wandering, Begging Monks,* 249–80.

Life of Aphu. Ed. E. Revillout. "La vie du bienheureux Aphou." *Revue Égyptologique* 3 (1883): 28–33.

Life of Isaac. Trans. Peter Hatlie. "The Encomium of Ss. Isakos and Dalmatos by Michael the Monk (BHG3 956d): Text, Translation and Notes." In *EUKOSMIA. Studi miscellanei per il 75° d. Vincenzo Poggi S.J.,* edited by V. Ruggieri and L. Pieralli. Soveria Mannelli (Catanzaro): Rubbettino, 2003. 275–311.

Life of Saint Auxentius. Ed. P. Varalda. *Vita sancti Auxentii (BHG 199).* Hellenica 64. Alessandria, Italy: Edizioni dell'Orso, 2017.

Pseudo-Macarius. *Spiritual Homilies.* Ed. H. Berthold. *Makarios/Symeon, Reden und Briefe. Die Sammlung I des Vaticanus Graecus 694 (B).* Die griechischen christlichen Schriftsteller der ersten Jahrhunderte 55 and 56. Berlin: Akademie-Verlag, 1973 (= Collection I); Ed. H. Dorries, E. Klostermann, and M. Kroeger. *Die 50 Geistlichen Homilien des Makarios.* Patristische Texte und Studien 4. Berlin:

De Gruyter, 1964, repr. 2010 (= Collection II [Homillies 1–50]); Ed. V. Desprez. *Pseudo-Macaire: Oeuvres spirituelles 1: Homélies propres à la Collection III*. Sources chrétiennes 275. Paris: Éditions du Cerf, 1980 (= Collection III]); Ed. R. Staats. *Makarios-Symeon: Epistola Magna. Eine messalianische Monchsregel und ihre Umschrift in Gregors von Nyssa "De Instituto Christiano."* Gottingen: Vandenhoeck & Ruprecht, 1984. Trans. George A. Mahoney. *Pseudo-Macarius: The Fifty Spiritual Homilies and the Great Letter*. The Classics of Western Spirituality. Mahwah: Paulist Press, 1992.

Origen. *Against Celsus*. Ed. M. Marcovich. *Origenes. Contra Celsum libri viii*. Supplements to Vigiliae Christianae 54. Leiden: Brill, 2001.

Origen. *On First Principles*. Ed. Henri Crouzel and Manlio Simonetti. *Origène. Traité des Principes. Tome I (Livres I et II)*. Sources chrétiennes 252. Paris: Éditions du Cerf, 1978.

Palladius of Helenopolis. *Lausiac History*. Ed. G. J. M. Bartelink. *Palladio. La storia lausica*. Vite dei Santi 2. N.p.: Lorenzo Valla, 1974.

Procopius of Caesarea. *History of the Wars*. Ed. G. Wirth. *Procopii Caesariensis opera omnia*. 2 vols. Leipzig: Teubner, 1962–1963.

Samuel. *The Life of the Syrian Saint Barsauma: Eulogy of a Hero of the Resistance to the Council of Chalcedon*. Trans. Andrew Palmer. Transformation of the Classical Heritage 61. Oakland: University of California Press, 2020.

Socrates. *Ecclesiastical History*. Ed. Günther Christian Hansen. *Sokrates. Kirchengeschichte*. Die Griechischen Christlichen Schriftsteller der Ersten Jahr neue Folge. Berlin: Akademie-Verlag, 1995.

Sozomen. *Ecclesiastical History*. Ed. and trans. Josef Bidez. *Sozomène. Histoire ecclésiastique*. Sources chrétiennes 306, 418, 495, 516. Paris: Éditions du Cerf, 1983, 1996, 2005, 2008.

Sulpicius Severus. *Life of Martin*. Ed. and trans. Philip Burton. *Sulpicius Severus' Vita Martini*. Oxford and New York: Oxford University Press, 2017.

Synaxarium of the Constantinopolitan Church, June 17.2. Ed. Hippolyte Delehaye. Brussels, 1902.

Theodoret of Cyrrhus. *Church History*. Ed. Günther Christian Hansen and Léon Parmentier. *Theodoret. Kirchengeschichte*. Die Griechischen Christlichen Schriftsteller der Ersten Jahr 5. Berlin: Akademie-Verlag, 1998.

Theodoret of Cyrrhus. *Religious History* (*Philotheos historia*). Ed. and trans. Pierre Canivet and Alice Leroy-Molinghen. *Histoire des moines de Syrie*. Sources chrétiennes 234 and 257. Paris: Éditions du Cerf, 1977, 1979.

Theodosian Code and Novels: And the Sirmondian Constitutions. Trans. Clyde Pharr. Princeton: Princeton University Press, 1952.

Secondary Sources

Adams, Sean A. *The Genre of Acts and Collected Biography*. Society for New Testament Monograph Series 156. Cambridge: Cambridge University Press, 2013.

Adams, Sean A. "What are *Bioi*/Vitae? Generic Self-Consciousness in Ancient Biography." In *The Oxford Handbook of Ancient Biography*, edited by Koen de Temmerman. Oxford: Oxford University Press, 2020. 19–31.

Barnes, Timothy D. *Early Christian Hagiography and Roman History*. 2nd rev. ed. Tübingen: Mohr Siebeck, 2016.

Bartelink, G. J. M. "Text Parallels between the Vita Hypatii of Callinicus and the Pseudo-Macariana." *Vigiliae Christianae* 22 (1968): 128–36.

Beck, Hans-Georg. *Kirche und theologische Literatur im byzantinischen Reich*. Byzantinisches Handbuch im Rahmen des Handbuchs der Altertumswissenschaft 2.1. Munich: C. H. Beck'sche Verlagsbuchhandlung, 1959.

Brakke, David. *Athanasius and the Politics of Asceticism*. Oxford Early Christian Studies. Oxford: Oxford University Press, 1992.

Brakke, David. *Demons and the Making of the Monk: Spiritual Combat in Early Christianity*. Cambridge: Harvard University Press, 2006.

Brown, Peter. "Christianization and Social Conflict." In *The Cambridge Ancient History. Volume XIII: The Late Empire, A.D. 337–425*, edited by Averil Cameron and Peter Garnsey. Cambridge: Cambridge University Press, 1998. 632–64.

Brown, Peter. "The Rise and Function of the Holy Man." *Journal of Roman Studies* 61 (1971): 80–101.

Brown, Peter. "The Rise and Function of the Holy Man, 1971–1997." *Journal of Early Christian Studies* 6 (1998): 353–76.

Browning, Robert. "The 'Low Level' Saint's Life in the Early Byzantine World." In *The Byzantine Saint*, edited by Sergei Hackel. Crestwood, NY: St Vladimir's Seminary Press, 2001. 117–27.

Cain, Andrew. *The Greek* Historia Monachorum in Aegypto: *Monastic Hagiography in the Late Fourth Century*. Oxford Early Christian Studies. Oxford: Oxford University Press, 2016.

Cameron, Alan. "Cyril of Scythopolis, V. Sabae 53: A Note on κατά in Late Greek." *Glotta* 56 (1978): 87–94.

Cameron, Averil. *Christianity and the Rhetoric of Empire: The Development of Christian Discourse*. Sather Classical Lectures 55. Berkeley: University of California Press, 1991.

Caner, Daniel. *Wandering, Begging Monks: Spiritual Authority and the Promotion of Monasticism in Late Antiquity*. Transformation of the Classical Heritage 33. Berkeley: University of California Press, 2002.

Clark, Elizabeth A. *The Origenist Controversy: The Cultural Construction of an Early Christian Debate*. Princeton: Princeton University Press, 1992.

Coon, Lynda L. *Sacred Fictions: Holy Women and Hagiography in Late Antiquity*. Middle Ages Series. Philadelphia: University of Pennsylvania Press, 1997.

Corke-Webster, James, and Christa Grey. "Introduction." In *The Hagiographical Experiment: Developing Discourses of Sainthood*, edited by James Corke-Webster and Christa Grey. Supplements to Vigiliae Christianae 158. Leiden: Brill, 2020. 1–26.

Dagron, Gilbert. "Le monachisme à Constantinople jusqu'au concile de Chalcédoine (451)." *Travaux et mémoires* 4 (1970): 229–76.

Dagron, Gilbert. *Vie et miracles de Sainte Thècle*. Subsidia Hagiographica 62. Brussels: Société des Bollandistes, 1978.

Delehaye, Hippolyte. "Byzantine Monasticism." In *Byzantium: An Introduction to East Roman Civilization*, edited by Norman H. Baynes and H. St. L. Moss. Oxford: Clarendon Press, 1948. 133–65.

Delehaye, Hippolyte. *Les légendes hagiographiques*. 2nd ed. Brussels: Bureaux de la Société des Bollandistes, 1906.

De Temmerman, Koen. "Writing (about) Ancient Lives: Scholarship, Definitions, and Concepts." In *The Oxford Handbook of Ancient*

Biography*, edited by Koen de Temmerman. Oxford: Oxford University Press, 2020. 3–18.

Efthymiadis, Stephanos, ed. *The Ashgate Research Companion to Byzantine Hagiography, Volume I: Periods and Places*. Ashgate Research Companions. London and New York: Routledge, 2011.

Efthymiadis, Stephanos, ed. *The Ashgate Research Companion to Byzantine Hagiography, Volume II: Genres and Contexts*. Ashgate Research Companions. London and New York: Routledge, 2014.

Elm, Susanna. *"Virgins of God": The Making of Asceticism in Late Antiquity*. Oxford Classical Monographs. Oxford: Clarendon Press, 1994.

Gaddis, Michael, and Richard Price. *The Acts of the Council of Chalcedon*. 3 vols. Translated Texts for Historians 45. Liverpool: Liverpool University Press, 2005.

Gibbon, Edward. *The History of the Decline and Fall of the Roman Empire, Volume II: A.D. 476–1461*. New York: The Modern Library, 1932.

Hanson, R. P. C. *The Search for the Christian Doctrine of God: The Arian Controversy, 318–381*. London and New York: T&T Clark, 1988.

Hatlie, Peter. *The Monks and Monasteries of Constantinople, ca. 350–850*. Cambridge: Cambridge University Press, 2007.

Holum, Kenneth. *Theodosian Empresses: Women and Imperial Dominion in Late Antiquity*. Transformation of the Classical Heritage 3. Berkeley: University of California Press, 1982.

Janin, Raymond. *Les églises et les monastères des grands centres byzantins (Bithynie, Hellespont, Latros, Galèsios, Trébizonde, Athènes, Thessalonique)*. Paris: Institut Français d'Études Byzantines, 1975.

Jiménez Sánchez, Juan Antonio. "The Monk Hypatius and the Olympic Games of Chalcedon." *Studia Patristica* 60 (2013): 39–45.

Jones, A. H. M., J. R. Martindale, and J. Morris. *The Prosopography of the Later Roman Empire: Volume 1, A.D. 260–395*. Cambridge: Cambridge University Press, 1971.

Krueger, Derek. *Writing as Holiness: The Practice of Holiness in the Early Christian East*. Divinations: Re-reading Late Ancient Religion. Philadelphia: University of Pennsylvania Press, 2004.

Leo, Friedrich. *Die griechisch römische Biographie nach ihrer litterarischen Form*. Leipzig: Teubner, 1901.

Mango, Cyril. "Diabolus Byzantinus." *Dumbarton Oaks Papers* 46 (1992): 215–23.

Mango, Cyril. "Saints." In *The Byzantines*, edited by Guglielmo Cavallo and translated by Thomas Dunlap, Teresa Lavender Fagan, and Charles Lambert. Chicago: University of Chicago Press, 1997. 255–80.

Martindale, J. R. *The Prosopography of the Later Roman Empire, Volume II: A.D. 395–527.* Cambridge: Cambridge University Press, 1980.

Maxwell, Jaclyn. "Social Interactions in a Rural Monastery: Scholars, Peasants, Monks, and More in the *Life of Hypatius.*" In *Motions of Late Antiquity: Essays on Religion, Politics, and Society in Honour of Peter Brown*, edited by Jamie Kreiner and Helmut Reimitz. Cultural Encounters in Late Antiquity and the Middle Ages 20. Turnhout: Brepols, 2018. 89–106.

Momigliano, Arnaldo. *The Development of Greek Biography.* Expanded ed. Cambridge, MA: Harvard University Press, 1993.

Pargoire, Jules. "Rufinianes." *Byzantinische Zeitschrift* 8 (1899): 429–77.

Plested, Marcus. *The Macarian Legacy: The Place of Macarius-Symeon in the Eastern Christian Tradition.* Oxford Theological Monographs. Oxford: Oxford University Press, 2004.

Przyszychowska, Marta. "The Date of the Council of Gangra Reconsidered (358)." *Journal of Early Christian Studies* 30 (2022): 223–43.

Rebenich, Stefan. "Inventing an Ascetic Hero: Jerome's *Life of Paul the Hermit.*" In *Jerome of Stridon: His Life, Writings and Legacy*, edited by Andrew Cain and Josef Lössl. London: Routledge, 2007. 13–27.

Rubenson, Samuel. "Antony and Pythagoras: A Reappraisal of the Appropriation of Classical Biography in Athanasius' *Vita Antonii.*" In *Beyond Reception: Mutual Influences between Antique Religion, Judaism, and Early Christianity*, edited by David Brakke, Anders-Christian Jacobsen, and Jörg Ulrich. Early Christianity in the Context of Antiquity 1. Frankfurt am Main: Peter Lang, 2006. 191–208.

Stewart, Columba. *"Working the Earth of the Heart": The Messalian Controversy in History, Texts, and Language to AD 431.* Oxford Theological Monographs. Oxford: Clarendon Press, 1991.

Storin, Bradley K. "Monastic Identity and Violence in Callinicus' *Vita Hypatii.*" *Studia Patristica* 129 (2021): 155–66.

Swain, Simon. "Biography and Biographic in the Literature of the Roman Empire." In *Portraits: Biographical Representation in the Greek and Latin Literature of the Roman Empire*, edited by Mark J. Edwards and Simon Swain. Oxford: Clarendon Press, 1997. 1–37.

Talbert, Richard J. A., ed. *Barrington Atlas of the Greek and Roman World*. Princeton: Princeton University Press, 2000.

Uytfanghe, Marc van. "L'hagiographie: un 'genre' chrétien ou antique tardif?" *Analecta Bollandiana* 111 (1993): 135–88.

Uytfanghe, Marc van. "L'origine et les ingredients du discours hagiographique." *Sacris Erudiri* 50 (2011): 35–70.

Veilleux, Arnaud. *Pachomian Koinonia, Volume One: The Life of Saint Pachomius and His Disciples*. Cistercian Studies 45. Kalamazoo, MI: Cistercian Publications, 1980.

Villecourt, Dom L. "La date et l'origine des 'Homélies Spirituelles' attribuées à Macaire." *Comptes rendus des sessions de l'Académie des Inscriptions et Belles-Lettres* 64, no. 3 (1920): 250–58.

Wölfle, Eugen. *Hypatios, Leben und Bedeutung des Abtes von Rufiniane*. Europäische Hochschulschriften 23. Frankfurt am Main: Peter Lang, 1986.

Index of Scriptural References and Citations

References are cited by page number.